IN THE
BEGINNING

26	25	24	23	22	21
6	5	4	3	2	1

WHEN WOMEN ARE
EQUIPPED WITH THE
KNOWLEDGE OF GOD'S
TRUTH, THE WORLD
IS TRANSFORMED ONE
WOMAN AT A TIME.

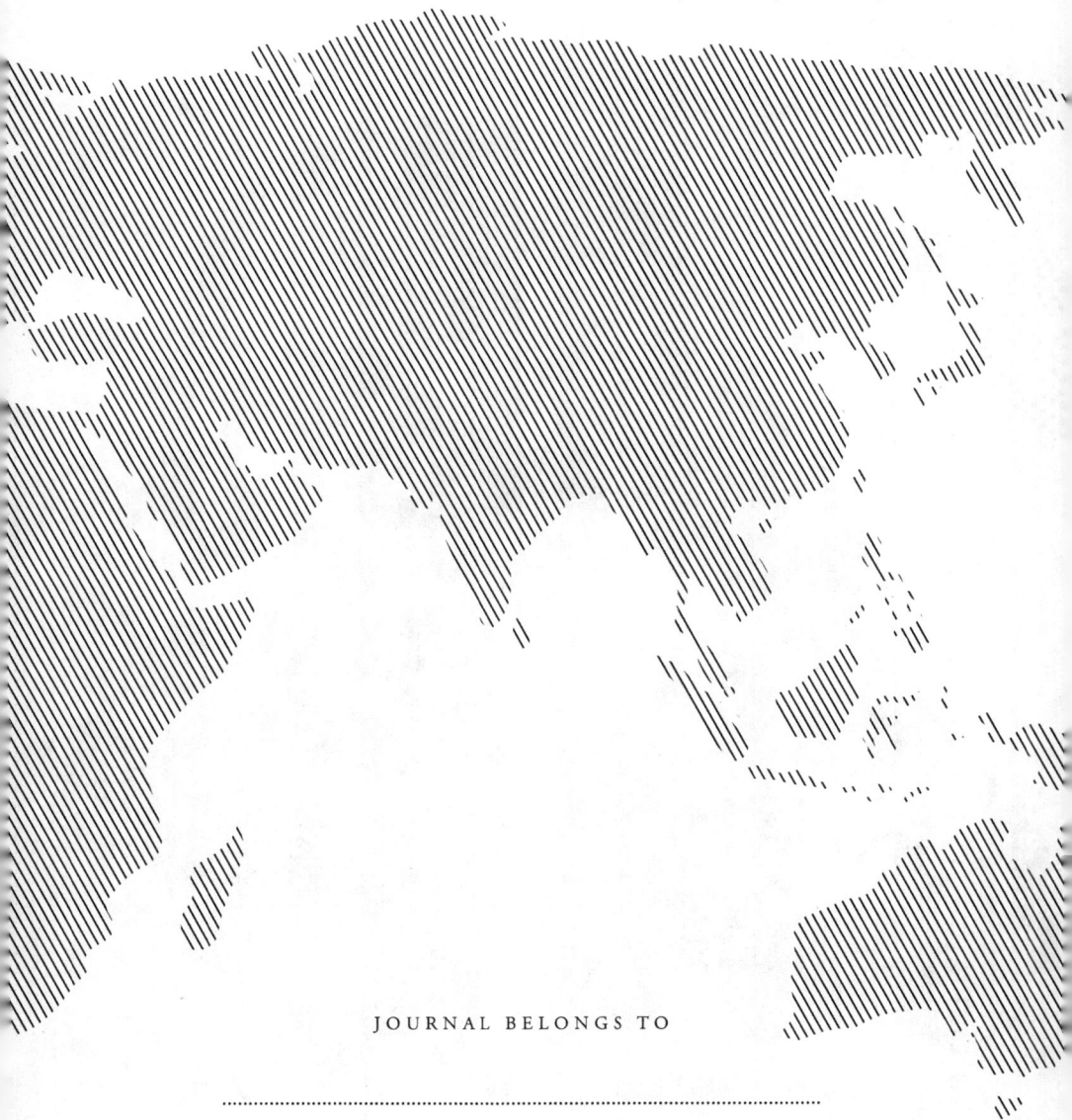

JOURNAL BELONGS TO

....

DATE

....

CONTENTS

You
HAVE BEEN
PRAYED FOR;
IT IS NOT A
COINCIDENCE
YOU ARE
PARTICIPATING
IN THIS
STUDY.

WELCOME FRIEND!

We are glad you have decided to join us in this Bible study! You have been prayed for; it is not a coincidence you are participating in this study.

Our prayer for you is simple: that you will grow closer to our Lord as you dig into His Word each and every day. Each day before you read the assigned passage, pray and ask God to help you understand it. Invite Him to speak to you through His Word. Then listen. Believe He will be faithful to speak to you, and be faithful to listen and obey.

Take time to read the verses over and over again. The Bible tells us that if we seek wisdom like silver, and search for it like hidden treasure, then we will understand how to fear the Lord, and we will discover knowledge about God (Prov 2:4-5).

All of us here at Love God Greatly can't wait for you to get started, and we hope to see you at the finish line. Endure, persevere, press on; don't give up! Finish well what you are beginning today.

We will be here every step of the way, cheering for you! We are in this together. Be expectant that God has much in store for you in this study. Journey with us as we learn to love God greatly with our lives!

WE NEED EACH OTHER, AND WE LIVE LIFE BETTER TOGETHER. WOULD YOU CONSIDER REACHING OUT AND DOING THIS STUDY WITH SOMEONE?

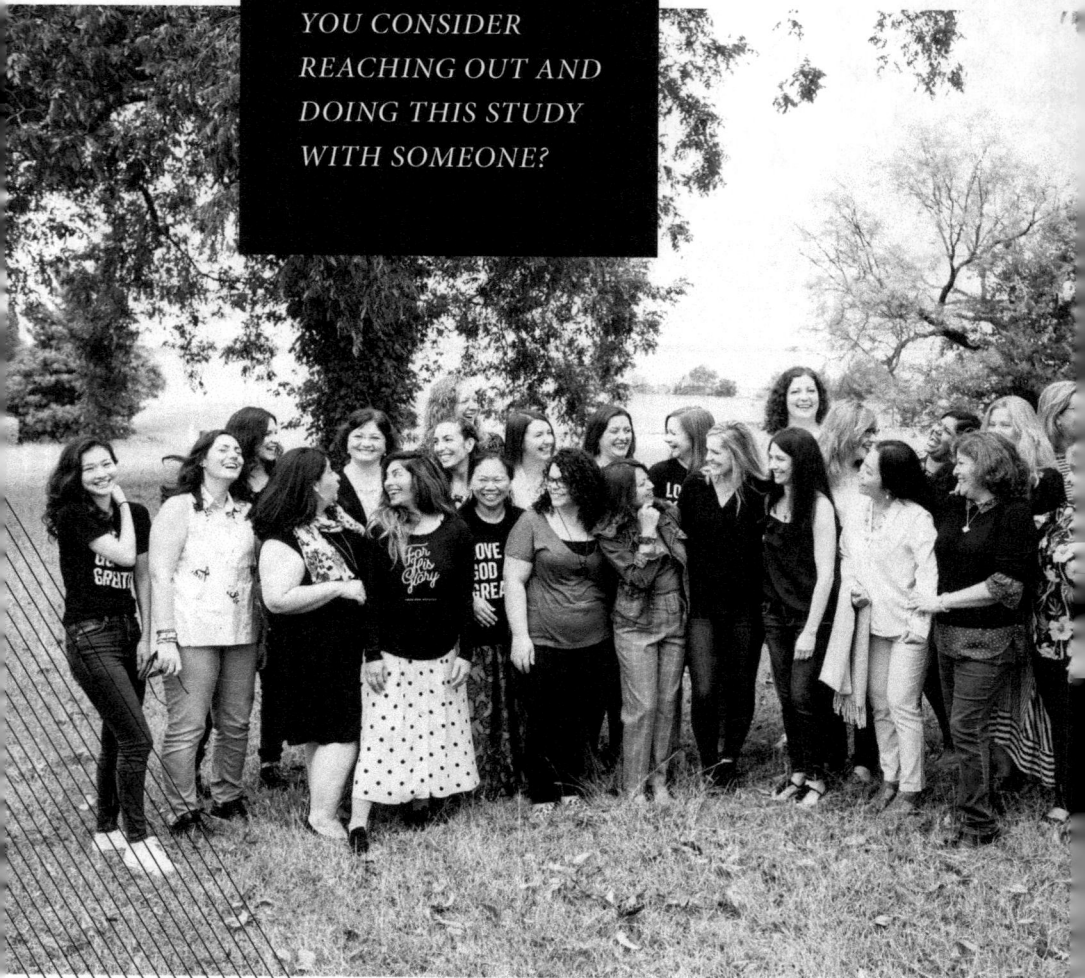

Love God Greatly exists to inspire, encourage, and equip women around the world to love God greatly with their lives.

INSPIRE women to make God's Word a priority in their daily lives through Bible study resources.

ENCOURAGE women in their walks with God through online community and personal accountability.

EQUIP women to grow in their faith so they can effectively reach others for Christ.

We start with a simple Bible reading plan, but it doesn't stop there. Some women gather in homes and churches locally, while others connect online with women across the globe, Whatever the method, we lovingly lock arms and unite for this purpose: to love God greatly with our lives.

At Love God Greatly, you'll find real, authentic women. You'll find women who desire less of each other, and a whole lot more of Jesus. Women who long to know God through His Word because we believe that truth transforms and sets us free. Women who are better together, saturated in God's Word and in community with one another.

Love God Greatly is committed to providing quality Bible study materials and believes finances should never get in the way of a woman being able to participate in one of our studies. All journals are available to download for free from LoveGodGreatly.com.

Our journals and books are also available for sale on Amazon. Search for "Love God Greatly" to see all of our Bible study journals and books.

YOU'LL FIND WOMEN WHO ARE IMPERFECT, YET FORGIVEN.

Love God Greatly is a 501 (C) (3) non-profit organization. Funding for Love God Greatly comes through donations and proceeds from our online Bible study journals and books.

One-hundred percent of proceeds go directly back into supporting Love God Greatly and helping us inspire, encourage, and equip women all over the world with God's Word.

Arm-in-arm and hand-in-hand, let's do this together.

THE NEED

Billions of women around the world don't have access to God's Word in their native language. Those who do, don't have access to women's Bible studies designed and written with them in mind.

THE MISSION

At Love God Greatly, we create Bible studies in 30+ languages. We equip missionaries, ministries, local churches, and women with God's Word at an unprecedented rate by allowing our journals to be downloaded from our international sites at no cost.

Through studying the Bible in their own language with like-minded communities, women are trained and equipped with God's Word.

We believe when women read and apply God's Word to their lives and embrace His unchanging love for them, the world is a better place. We know one woman in God's Word can change a family, a community, and a nation... one woman at a time.

PARTNER WITH US

We would love for you to join us in our mission of giving women all over the world access to God's Word and quality Bible study resources! For any questions or for more information, email us or visit us online. We would love to hear from you!

INFO@LOVEGODGREATLY.COM

LOVEGODGREATLY.COM

AT LOVE GOD GREATLY,
WE CREATE BIBLE STUDIES
IN 30+ LANGUAGES.

A t Love God Greatly, we believe that the Word of God is living and active. The words of Scripture are powerful and effective and relevant for life in all times and all cultures. In order to interpret the Bible correctly, we need an understanding of the context and culture of the original writings.

As we study the Bible, we use the SOAP Bible Study Method. The acronym stands for Scripture, Observation, Application, and Prayer. It's one thing simply to read Scripture. When you interact with it, intentionally slowing down to reflect, truths start jumping off the page. The SOAP Method allows us to dig deeper into Scripture and see more than we would if we simply read the verses. It allows us not only to be hearers of the Word, but doers as well (Jas 1:22).

YOU WILL NEVER WASTE TIME IN GOD'S WORD. IT IS LIVING, POWERFUL, AND EFFECTIVE, AND HE SPEAKS TO US THROUGH IT.

In this journal, we read a passage of Scripture and then apply the SOAP Method to specific verses. Using this method allows us to glean a greater understanding of Scripture, which allows us to apply it effectively to our lives.

The most important ingredients in the SOAP Method are your interaction with God's Word and your application of it to your life. Take time to study it carefully, discovering the truth of God's character and heart for the world.

Studying God's Word can be challenging and even confusing. We use the SOAP method to help us simplify our study and focus on key passages.

SOAP

Bible Study Method

S

**STANDS FOR
SCRIPTURE**

*Physically write out
the SOAP verses.*

*You'll be amazed at what
God will reveal to you
just by taking the time to
slow down and write out
what you are reading!*

SOAP

WEEK 1 • MONDAY

SCRIPTURE / *Write out the SOAP verses*

Then I heard a loud voice in heaven saying, "The salvation
and the power and the kingdom of our God, and the
ruling authority of his Christ, have now come, because the
accuser of our brothers and sisters, the one who accuses
them day and night before our God, has been thrown
down. Revelation 12:10

But the Lord is faithful, and he will strengthen you and
protect you from the evil one. 2 Thessalonians 3:3

OBSERVATION / *Write 3 - 4 observations*

Loud voice, powerful, all knowing
We are accused day and night, constant struggle
The Lord will help, establish and guard me
He's always there
He's is constant, a protector in my life, guardian

O

**STANDS FOR
OBSERVATION**

*What do you see in the
verses that you're reading?*

*Who is the intended
audience? Is there a
repetition of words?*

*What words stand
out to you?*

A
STANDS FOR
APPLICATION

This is when God's Word becomes personal.

What is God saying to you today? How can you apply what you just read to your own personal life?

What changes do you need to make? Is there action you need to take?

APPLICATION / *Write down 1 - 2 applications*

Remind myself of God's strength is more powerful than anything
Memorize these verses and say them daily this week
Ask God to strengthen my faith in Him
Trust God that he will deliver me from evil
Pray for my brothers and sister's in Christ

PRAYER / *Write out a prayer over what you learned*

Dear Lord,

Thank you for being constant, faithful, and loving towards me
and my life. Help me to further my trust and faith in you
daily and through difficult times.

Help me to know you're alway there by my side, guarding,
and protecting me. Remind me of the suffering of others and
to be able to help and encourage them in their growth.

I ask all these things in Jesus name.
Amen

P
STANDS FOR PRAYER

Pray God's Word back to Him.
Spend time thanking Him.

If He has revealed something to you during this time in His Word, pray about it.

If He has revealed some sin that is in your life, confess. And remember, He loves you dearly.

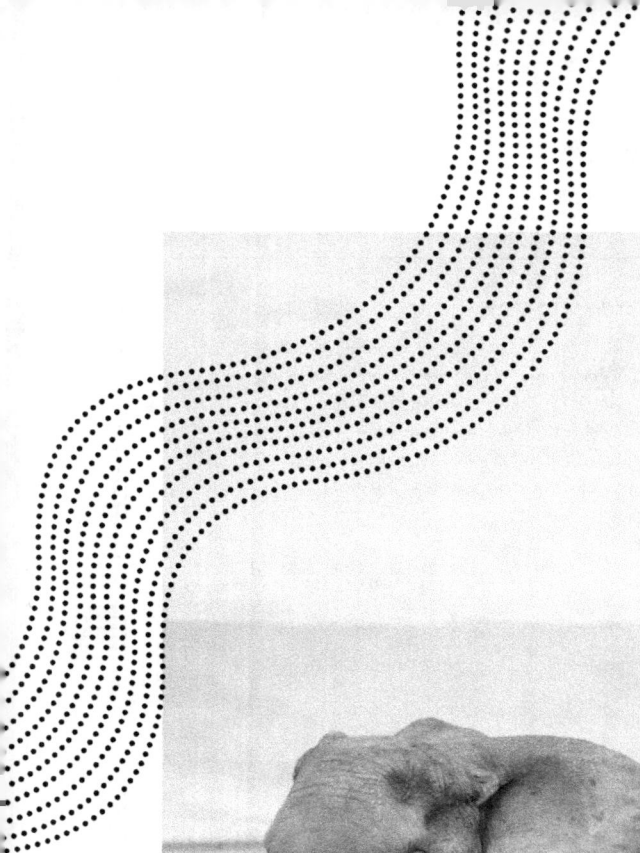

As a child, I was rushed to the hospital after I swallowed a coin and it got stuck in my throat. I was scheduled to have an operation the next day because, by the time I arrived at the hospital, the coin was stuck between my ribs. That same night, I woke up and felt something in my mouth. I reached in and the coin had miraculously come out! I knew then God was with me, and He has been with me through much more!

MY LIFE IS RICHER BECAUSE OF THIS WONDERFUL COMMUNITY.

I gave my life to Christ in my teens and, since then, the longing of my heart has been to live fully for Him. I am grateful for my parents who trained me in the ways of God. I married a wonderful, God-fearing man in my mid-twenties and we have been blessed with three beautiful children.

We relocated to Australia in 2014. After coming to Australia, I couldn't find an in-depth Bible study group to join. It was challenging to find one that worked with the schedule of my growing family, so I started searching for an online Bible study. I found Love God Greatly in 2017, where I joined the 1 & 2 Timothy study.

I love using the Love God Greatly studies because I can do in-depth Bible studies at my leisure and connect with women from different parts of the world. The SOAP method challenges me to apply what I have been reading and helps me gain wisdom and understanding. My life is richer because of this wonderful community. I've been privileged to be part of the LGG encouragement team and translators team. God has enabled me to work with my beautiful East African sisters to translate the studies into Swahili. As a child and growing up, I always felt like God was with me. I'm blessed to share this hope and encouragement with women around the world. I am grateful for the gift of life and salvation.

Manoti
LGG Swahili Branch

LANGUAGE
Swahili

GLOBAL
SPEAKERS
3,932,000

TO CONNECT WITH THIS BRANCH
lggswahilibranch@gmail.com

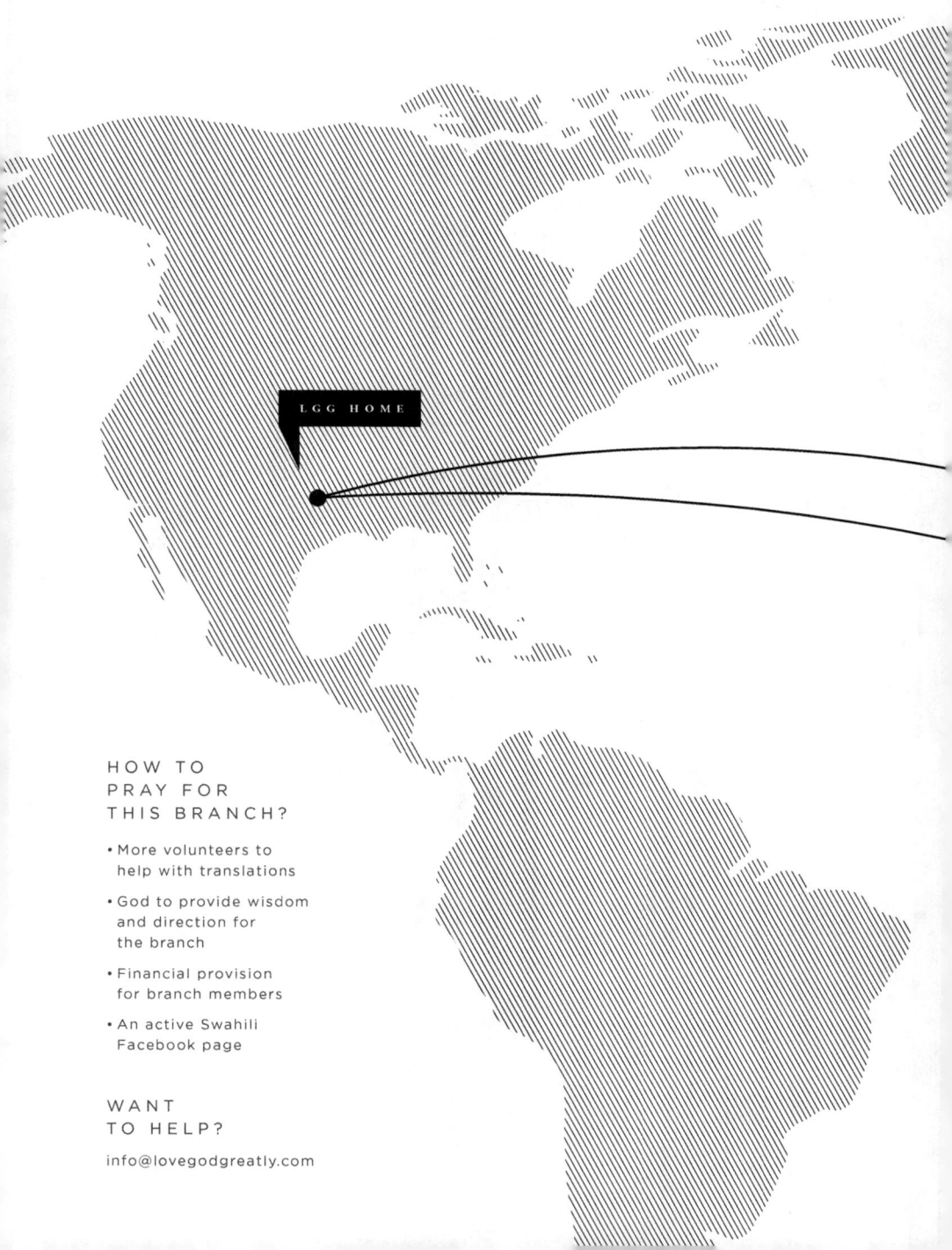

LGG HOME

HOW TO PRAY FOR THIS BRANCH?

- More volunteers to help with translations

- God to provide wisdom and direction for the branch

- Financial provision for branch members

- An active Swahili Facebook page

WANT TO HELP?

info@lovegodgreatly.com

GLOBAL OUTREACH

LGG Swahili Branch

Do you know someone
who could use our
Love God Greatly
Bible studies in the
Swahili language?

If so, make sure and
tell them all the
amazing Bible study
resources we provide
to help equip them
with God's Word!

UGANDA

DEMOCRATIC
REPUBLIC
OF CONGO

KENYA

TANZANIA

COMOROS ISLANDS

Chicken Pilau

INGREDIENTS

4 TABLESPOON OLIVE OIL

3 RED ONIONS, SLICED

½ TEASPOON GROUND CUMIN

½ TEASPOON GROUND CORIANDER

¼ TEASPOON GROUND CINNAMON

⅛ TEASPOON GROUND CARDAMOM

1 TEASPOON GINGER

1 TEASPOON TOMATO PASTE

2 MEDIUM GARLIC CLOVES, GRATED

3 LBS BONE-IN CHICKEN DRUMSTICKS OR THIGH, SKIN RE-
MOVED (CHICKEN CAN BE SUBSTITUTED WITH BEEF OR LAMB)

1 CUP UNCOOKED BASMATI RICE

2 CUPS CHICKEN STOCK

SALT & PEPPER

DIRECTIONS

Heat the oil in a Dutch oven over medium-high heat. Add sliced onion to the pan and cook, stirring occasionally, until onions are lightly browned, about 4 minutes. Add the cumin, coriander, cinnamon, cardamom, ginger, and garlic to the pan and stir to combine.

Generously season the chicken pieces with salt and pepper (optional). Cook the chicken in the onion and spices, stirring occasionally, for about 10 minutes.

Add the rice and ½ tsp of salt to the pan, stir to combine. Slowly pour in the chicken stock and scrape the bottom and sides of the pan with a wooden spoon or spatula to release any stuck-on bits. Bring to a boil.

Cover the Dutch oven tightly with a lid and reduce heat to low. Cook with the lid on, on low heat for 20 minutes. Take it off the heat and let the pilau rest 15 minutes ensuring the lid is still on.

Season with salt and pepper to taste.

KNOW THESE TRUTHS

GOD LOVES YOU

God's Word says, "For this is the way God loved the world: He gave his one and only Son, so that everyone who believes in him will not perish but have eternal life" (John 3:16).

OUR SIN SEPARATES US FROM GOD

We are all sinners by nature and by choice, and because of this we are separated from God, who is holy. God's Word says, "for all have sinned and fall short of the glory of God" (Rom 3:23).

JESUS DIED SO YOU MIGHT HAVE LIFE

The consequence of sin is death, but God's free gift of salvation is available to us. Jesus took the penalty for our sin when He died on the cross.

God's Word says, "For the payoff of sin is death, but the gift of God is eternal life in Christ Jesus our Lord" (Rom 6:23); "But God demonstrates his own love for us, in that while we were still sinners, Christ died for us" (Rom 5:8).

JESUS LIVES!

Death could not hold Him, and three days after His body was placed in the tomb Jesus rose again, defeating sin and death forever. He lives today in heaven and is preparing a place in eternity for all who believe in Him.

Jesus says, "There are many dwelling places in my Father's house. Otherwise, I would have told you, because I am going away to make ready a place for you. And if I go and make ready a place for you, I will come again and take you to be with me, so that where I am you may be too" (John 14:2–3).

KNOW YOU CAN BE FORGIVEN

Accepting Jesus as your Savior is not about what you can do, but rather about having faith in what Jesus has already done. It takes recognizing that you are a sinner, believing that Jesus died for your sins, and asking for forgiveness by placing your full trust in Jesus' work on the cross on your behalf.

God's Word says, "if you confess with your mouth that Jesus is Lord and believe in your heart that God raised him from the dead, you will be saved. For with the heart one believes and thus has righteousness and with the mouth one confesses and thus has salvation" (Rom 10:9–10).

ACCEPT CHRIST'S FREE GIFT OF SALVATION

Practically, what does that look like? With a sincere heart, you can pray a simple prayer like this:

Jesus,
I know that I am a sinner. I don't want to live another day without embracing the love and forgiveness that You have for me. I ask for Your forgiveness. I believe that You died for my sins and rose from the dead. I surrender all that I am and ask You to be Lord of my life. Help me to turn from my sin and follow You. Teach me what it means to walk in freedom as I live under Your grace, and help me to grow in Your ways as I seek to know You more. Amen.

CONNECT AND GROW

If you just prayed this prayer (or something similar in your own words) we'd love to connect with you!

You can email us at info@lovegodgreatly.com. We'd love to celebrate with you, pray with you, and help you connect to a local church. We are here to encourage you as you begin your new life as a child of God.

Let's Begin

IN THE BEGINNING

Introduction

The first eleven chapters of Genesis can be challenging to understand. While there is much debate in the world today about the true meaning of these events, we can rest in the truth that God's Word provides us with exactly what we need to be equipped for good works (2 Timothy 3:17), even in our questions. The Book of Genesis as a whole displays the character of God; His kindness, creativity, holiness, justice, wrath, power, and majesty are clearly portrayed on every page.

Genesis 1–11 describes the way God created the world. These chapters were written to illuminate the holiness of God and show how humankind carries His image. They show God's faithfulness to those who followed Him and the way He dealt with those who, in rebellion, turned from His ways. God's creativity is on display in the creation story, His holiness seen when He deals with sin, His compassion evident when He cares for His people, His power and authority over creation shown through the flood, and His grace demonstrated in His promise of future redemption for sinful humans.

Most evangelical scholars agree that Genesis was written by Moses during the time the Israelites wandered in the Desert of Zin, around 1440 B.C.

Written to the generation of Israelites preparing to enter and live in the Promised Land of Canaan, the words of Genesis reminded them who their God is and what it looked like to walk with Him.

HIS KINDNESS, CREATIVITY, HOLINESS, JUSTICE, WRATH, POWER, AND MAJESTY ARE CLEARLY PORTRAYED ON EVERY PAGE.

In this Bible study, we will explore the first eleven chapters of Genesis, discovering the beginnings of creation, sin, grace, redemption, and promise. We can learn to love God greatly by studying His character, especially the aspects that are challenging and raise more questions in our faith. God shows His power and love in how He interacts with humanity. God is faithful to His people, His promises, and His covenant. His creativity is on display, reminding us of the vastness of His ability. May we be open to learn all He has for us, expectant that He will reveal Himself to us in new ways as we seek Him.

WEEK 1

○ *Monday*
Read: Genesis 1:1-5; Job 38:4-7
SOAP: Genesis 1:3-4

○ *Tuesday*
Read: Genesis 1:6-8; Job 38:19-30
SOAP: Job 38:25-27

○ *Wednesday*
Read: Genesis 1:9-13; Job 38:8-11
SOAP: Genesis 1:9-10

○ *Thursday*
Read: Genesis 1:14-19; Job 38:12-18; 31-35
SOAP: Job 38:12-13

○ *Friday*
Read: Genesis 1:20-23; Job 39:26-30
SOAP: Job 39:26-27

WEEK 2

○ *Monday*
Read: Genesis 1:24-31; Job 39:1-12
SOAP: Genesis 1:27

○ *Tuesday*
Read: Genesis 2:1-3; Exodus 20:8-11; Mark 2:27
SOAP: Exodus 20:11

○ *Wednesday*
Read: Genesis 2:4-7; Psalm 8:4-6
SOAP: Psalm 8:5-6

○ *Thursday*
Read: Genesis 2:8-14; Isaiah 58:11-12
SOAP: Genesis 2:8-9

○ *Friday*
Read: Genesis 2:15-17; Psalm 19:7-11
SOAP: Psalm 19:7-8

Check it off

WEEK 3

○ *Monday*
Read: Genesis 2:18-25; Matthew 19:4-6
SOAP: Matthew 19:4-6

○ *Tuesday*
Read: Genesis 3:1-7; 1 Peter 5:8-9
SOAP: 1 Peter 5:8-9

○ *Wednesday*
Read: Genesis 3:8-19; Romans 5:20-21
SOAP: Romans 5:20-21

○ *Thursday*
Read: Genesis 3:20-24; Ephesians 2:4-10
SOAP: Ephesians 2:8

○ *Friday*
Read: Genesis 4:1-16; Psalm 51:17; Hosea 6:6
SOAP: Hosea 6:6

WEEK 4

○ *Monday*
Read: Genesis 4:17-26; Psalm 150
SOAP: Psalm 150:1-6

○ *Tuesday*
Read: Genesis 5:1-32; Psalm 39:4-6
SOAP: Genesis 5:24

○ *Wednesday*
Read: Genesis 6:1-8; Romans 3:21-26
SOAP: Romans 3:23-24

○ *Thursday*
Read: Genesis 6:9-22; Hebrews 11:7
SOAP: Hebrews 11:7

○ *Friday*
Read: Genesis 7:1-24; Psalm 23
SOAP: Psalm 23:4

WEEK 5

○ *Monday*
Read: Genesis 8:1-14; Psalm 29:10-11
SOAP: Psalm 29:10-11

○ *Tuesday*
Read: Genesis 8:15-22; Psalm 115:16-18
SOAP: Psalm 115:16-18

○ *Wednesday*
Read: Genesis 9:1-17; 2 Corinthians 1:20-22
SOAP: Genesis 9:12-13

○ *Thursday*
Read: Genesis 9:18-29; Exodus 13:3-5
SOAP: Genesis 9:26

○ *Friday*
Read: Genesis 10:1-7; Acts 17:26
SOAP: Acts 17:26

WEEK 6

○ *Monday*
Read: Genesis 10:8-20; Jonah 3
SOAP: Jonah 3:10

○ *Tuesday*
Read: Genesis 10:21-32; Proverbs 19:23
SOAP: Proverbs 19:23

○ *Wednesday*
Read: Genesis 11:1-9; Isaiah 55:8-9
SOAP: Isaiah 55:8-9

○ *Thursday*
Read: Genesis 11:10-26; Matthew 1:1-17
SOAP: Matthew 1:16

○ *Friday*
Read: Genesis 11:27-32; Psalm 139:13-16
SOAP: Psalm 139:16

YOUR GOALS

Write three goals you would like to focus on as you begin each day and dig into God's Word. Make sure you refer back to these goals throughout the next weeks to help you stay focused. You can do it!

ONE

....
....
....
....
....
....
....

TWO

....
....
....
....
....
....
....

THREE

....
....
....
....
....
....

God said, "Let there be light." And there was light! God saw that the light was good, so God separated the light from the darkness.

Genesis 1:3-4

PRAY

*Write down your prayer requests
and praises for this week.*

....

....

....

....

....

....

....

....

....

....

....

....

WEEKLY CHALLENGE

*Spend time this week enjoying God's creation. If you can, spend time away from
anything human-made. Listen to the sounds of nature. Enjoy His creation without
capturing it with a photograph. What do you learn about God by observing creation?*

....

....

....

....

....

....

....

READ

Genesis 1:1-5

1 In the beginning God created the heavens and the earth.

2 Now the earth was without shape and empty, and darkness was over the surface of the watery deep, but the Spirit of God was moving over the surface of the water. 3 God said, "Let there be light." And there was light! 4 God saw that the light was good, so God separated the light from the darkness. 5 God called the light "day" and the darkness "night." There was evening, and there was morning, marking the first day.

Job 38:4-7

4 "Where were you when I laid the foundation of the earth? Tell me, if you possess understanding. 5 Who set its measurements—if you know— or who stretched a measuring line across it? 6 On what were its bases set, or who laid its cornerstone— 7 when the morning stars sang in chorus, and all the sons of God shouted for joy?

SOAP / *Genesis 1:3-4*
SCRIPTURE / *Write out the SOAP verses*

_____

_____

_____

_____

_____

_____

_____

_____

_____

_____

_____

_____

_____

_____

_____

_____

_____

_____

OBSERVATION / *Write 3 - 4 observations*

_____

_____

_____

_____

_____

_____

_____

APPLICATION / *Write down 1 - 2 applications*

_____
_____
_____
_____
_____
_____
_____
_____
_____
_____
_____

PRAYER / *Write out a prayer over what you learned*

_____
_____
_____
_____
_____
_____
_____
_____
_____
_____
_____
_____
_____
_____
_____
_____

SOAP

Genesis 1:3–4

God said, "Let there be light." And there was light! God saw that the light was good, so God separated the light from the darkness.

INTO THE TEXT

In the beginning, the earth was dark. It had no shape and contained only water. But God was there. He existed within the darkness, even before He created the light.

"Let there be light." God commanded light into existence. He changed the darkness by creating light. He separated light and dark, giving each a name. Scripture doesn't say the darkness was bad, but it does say God separated it from the light, which He said was good.

The creation of light also ushered in the creation of time as we understand it. Scripture doesn't talk about God specifically creating time, but with the introduction of light, God created days. Light marked the day and darkness marked the night. The change of light is how we measure time.

God created the earth with great intentionality, creativity, and purpose. Not one action of God in creation was a mistake. God laid the foundations of the earth, light and darkness, day and night, with purpose and meaning.

In the book of Job we find a few more details about God's intent and creativity in creation. Job was a righteous man who suffered terrible losses. Job did not sin by cursing God in the midst of his loss. However, he did ask God for some kind of explanation for his suffering. God responded by asking Job, in many ways, "Where were you when I . . . ?" The questions reminded Job of God's sovereignty.

When our world crumbles, we, like Job, can approach God's throne. We can pour our questions and pain out to Him. He may not always answer us how we hope, but we can rest in His sovereignty. He created the foundations of the earth, along with everything in it. He created light and time, and nothing is beyond His control. May we shout for joy as His people.

PRAYER

Lord God, I am amazed at Your power in creation. You created light and separated it from the darkness. I praise You for Your creativity, intentionality, and purpose in creation. Help me trust You when I feel overwhelmed by darkness. Amen.

READ

Genesis 1:6-8

6 God said, "Let there be an expanse in the midst of the waters and let it separate water from water." 7 So God made the expanse and separated the water under the expanse from the water above it. It was so. 8 God called the expanse "sky." There was evening, and there was morning, a second day.

Job 38:19-30

19 "In what direction does light reside, and darkness, where is its place, 20 that you may take them to their borders and perceive the pathways to their homes? 21 You know, for you were born before them; and the number of your days is great! 22 Have you entered the storehouse of the snow, or seen the armory of the hail, 23 which I reserve for the time of trouble, for the day of war and battle? 24 In what direction is lightning dispersed, or the east winds scattered over the earth? 25 Who carves out a channel for the heavy rains, and a path for the rumble of thunder, 26 to cause it to rain on an uninhabited land, a wilderness where there are no human beings, 27 to satisfy a devastated and desolate land, and to cause it to sprout with vegetation? 28 Does the rain have a father, or who has fathered the drops of the dew? 29 From whose womb does the ice emerge, and the frost from the sky, who gives birth to it, 30 when the waters become hard like stone, when the surface of the deep is frozen solid?

SOAP / *Job 38:25-27*
SCRIPTURE / *Write out the SOAP verses*

_____

_____

_____

_____

_____

_____

_____

_____

_____

_____

_____

_____

_____

_____

_____

_____

_____

_____

_____

OBSERVATION / *Write 3 - 4 observations*

_____

_____

_____

_____

_____

_____

APPLICATION / *Write down 1 - 2 applications*

_____

_____

_____

_____

_____

_____

_____

_____

_____

_____

PRAYER / *Write out a prayer over what you learned*

_____

_____

_____

_____

_____

_____

_____

_____

_____

_____

_____

_____

_____

_____

SOAP

Job 38:25–27

Who carves out a channel for the heavy rains, and a path for the rumble of thunder, to cause it to rain on an uninhabited land, a wilderness where there are no human beings, to satisfy a devastated and desolate land, and to cause it to sprout with vegetation?

INTO THE TEXT

On the second day, God created the sky. Sky can seem like a strange thing to create, as to us, it appears as empty space. God had great intentionality when He created the sky, using it as a way to separate water from water. God separated the water into what we now call "sea" and "atmosphere."

The sky is much more than empty space. God's power and creativity are displayed there each and every day. The sky is the place where darkness and light live. Each morning and each evening God creates sunrises and sunsets that are perfectly unique not only to each day, but to each location on earth. Oh the wonder of God's imagination!

The sky is also home to snow, hail, lightning, wind, rain, and thunder. When God questioned Job He showed more of His intent and purpose for each of these elements of nature. Snow and hail are reserved for times of battle. Lightning is directed in specific places. Rain is sent to water a parched wilderness.

God had a plan when He created the sky. He created the elements of wind and rain and weather for distinct purposes. And He sustains each one by His hand. He is behind the weather, behind the movement of storms and the changing of seasons. No act of nature occurs outside of His approval.

If God can be trusted to create and sustain the sky and the weather, with all its details and intricacies, how much more can He be trusted to sustain us in our moment of need? We can trust His character in any circumstance, crisis, or moment of victory. If He has a plan for the rain, He certainly has a plan for you and me.

PRAYER

Father God, You are mighty and powerful. I am in awe of the way You sustain and create. You have a plan for everything in creation, even each drop of rain. Help me trust You with my life and the things that overwhelm me. Help me surrender these things to You. Amen.

READ

Genesis 1:9-13

9 God said, "Let the water under the sky be gathered to one place and let dry ground appear." It was so. 10 God called the dry ground "land" and the gathered waters he called "seas." God saw that it was good.

11 God said, "Let the land produce vegetation: plants yielding seeds and trees on the land bearing fruit with seed in it, according to their kinds." It was so. 12 The land produced vegetation—plants yielding seeds according to their kinds, and trees bearing fruit with seed in it according to their kinds. God saw that it was good. 13 There was evening, and there was morning, a third day.

Job 38:8-11

8 "Who shut up the sea with doors when it burst forth, coming out of the womb, 9 when I made the storm clouds its garment, and thick darkness its swaddling band, 10 when I prescribed its limits, and set in place its bolts and doors, 11 when I said, 'To here you may come and no farther, here your proud waves will be confined'?

SOAP / *Genesis 1:9-10*
SCRIPTURE / *Write out the SOAP verses*

_____

_____

_____

_____

_____

_____

_____

_____

_____

_____

_____

_____

_____

_____

_____

_____

_____

_____

_____

_____

OBSERVATION / *Write 3 - 4 observations*

_____

_____

_____

_____

_____

_____

APPLICATION / *Write down 1 - 2 applications*

PRAYER / *Write out a prayer over what you learned*

SOAP

Genesis 1:9–10

God said, "Let the water under the sky be gathered to one place and let dry ground appear." It was so. God called the dry ground "land" and the gathered waters he called "seas." God saw that it was good.

INTO THE TEXT

On the third day of creation God gave shape to the earth. The earth had been only water, from what we can understand from Genesis 1:1. God first split the waters in two, creating the sky. God placed some water in the sky and some water on the earth.

On the third day God split the waters on the earth into seas, creating dry land. God gave boundaries to the water, instructing it on where it should go and where it was to be contained. God gave limits to the waves, creating dry land.

In biblical times, even into the first century, the sea was considered to be a place of darkness. They did not have the kind of equipment we have today, and crossing water was difficult, often deadly. There were even fish large enough to swallow a person whole (Jonah 1:17)! This gives us a greater understanding of the intense fear Jesus' disciples felt when they faced storms on the Sea of Galilee. Seas were unknown, frightening places where many lost their lives.

But God said the sea was good. God created the sea with a purpose, just like He created the sky and all its elements with a purpose, just like He created the dry land with vegetation and fruit for a purpose.

It can be tempting to look at the "seas" in our own lives, the trials, temptations, hardship, and pain, with much fear. We don't know how things will turn out. Much is out of our control and it can be easy to forget God's care and provision for us when we are overwhelmed with fear. In the same way God created the seas with purpose, every circumstance in our life has great purpose. God has not abandoned us, and He is still in control.

He set limits for the waves; He cares about the details of our lives.

PRAYER

Father God, You are sovereign over all creation, even the limits of each and every wave. You created the sea with purpose, and You have a purpose for everything You allow in my life. Give me patience to wait on Your timing and Your plan when I am fearful and uncertain. I believe You are with me. Amen.

READ

Genesis 1:14-19

14 God said, "Let there be lights in the expanse of the sky to separate the day from the night, and let them be signs to indicate seasons and days and years, 15 and let them serve as lights in the expanse of the sky to give light on the earth." It was so. 16 God made two great lights—the greater light to rule over the day and the lesser light to rule over the night. He made the stars also. 17 God placed the lights in the expanse of the sky to shine on the earth, 18 to preside over the day and the night, and to separate the light from the darkness. God saw that it was good. 19 There was evening, and there was morning, a fourth day.

Job 38:12-18; 31-35

12 Have you ever in your life commanded the morning, or made the dawn know its place, 13 that it might seize the corners of the earth, and shake the wicked out of it? 14 The earth takes shape like clay under a seal; its features are dyed like a garment. 15 Then from the wicked the light is withheld, and the arm raised in violence is broken. 16 Have you gone to the springs that fill the sea, or walked about in the recesses of the deep? 17 Have the gates of death been revealed to you? Have you seen the gates of deepest darkness? 18 Have you considered the vast expanses of the earth? Tell me, if you know it all.

31 Can you tie the bands of the Pleiades, or release the cords of Orion? 32 Can you lead out the constellations in their seasons, or guide the Bear with its cubs? 33 Do you know the laws of the heavens, or can you set up their rule over the earth? 34 Can you raise your voice to the clouds so that a flood of water covers you? 35 Can you send out lightning bolts, and they go? Will they say to you, 'Here we are'?

SOAP

WEEK 1 • THURSDAY

SOAP / *Job 38:12-13*
SCRIPTURE / *Write out the SOAP verses*

_____

_____

_____

_____

_____

_____

_____

_____

_____

_____

_____

_____

_____

_____

_____

_____

_____

_____

OBSERVATION / *Write 3 - 4 observations*

_____

_____

_____

_____

_____

_____

_____

APPLICATION / *Write down 1 - 2 applications*

_____

_____

_____

_____

_____

_____

_____

_____

_____

_____

PRAYER / *Write out a prayer over what you learned*

_____

_____

_____

_____

_____

_____

_____

_____

_____

_____

_____

_____

_____

_____

_____

SOAP

Job 38:12–13

Have you ever in your life commanded the morning, or made the dawn know its place, that it might seize the corners of the earth, and shake the wicked out of it?

INTO THE TEXT

One of the most beautiful places in the world to watch the sunrise is atop a volcano on the island of Maui, Hawai'i. Haleakalā is a dormant volcano, standing at 10,023 feet above sea level at the summit. The best way to watch the sunrise is to arrive before dawn, watching the blackness of the night give way to the glorious colors of the morning.

From 10,023 feet, the summit is dark and cold through the night. The stars and moon shine brilliantly, with the summit standing above any clouds that may inhibit the view. The first thread of light illuminates the horizon, turning the blackness into a navy blue. With the moon and stars still in view, the darkness slowly turns shades of blue, pink, and yellow as the sun inches toward the horizon. The clouds that sit below the summit roll and fold under the emerging light.

Finally, a great burst of yellow and white light illuminates everything in its path as the sun peaks over the horizon. Every moment, more light emerges, changing everything. The earth is illuminated, showing the vastness of the volcanic landscape. The clouds begin to break and offer glimpses of the ocean and the volcanic peaks on the island of Hawai'i. After such an experience one can't help but remember God's words to Job: "Have you ever in your life commanded the morning, or made the dawn know its place?"

God created the sun, moon, and stars with a specific purpose. They are signals of time and seasons, they provide light on the earth, and they separate light from darkness. Every morning, God reminds us of His sovereignty and character. Whether we view the dawn of the morning from atop a volcano or from the light coming into our homes, our God has still commanded that morning. He is in control each and every day. And without fail, He provides a new morning with new reminders of His love and faithfulness each and every day.

PRAYER

Lord God, I praise You for Your incredible power and creativity. You command each morning. You alone tell the dawn when to break. You bring light to the world, and You bring light to my life. Help me see Your incredible faithfulness today. Amen.

READ

Genesis 1:20-23

20 God said, "Let the water swarm with swarms of living creatures and let birds fly above the earth across the expanse of the sky." 21 God created the great sea creatures and every living and moving thing with which the water swarmed, according to their kinds, and every winged bird according to its kind. God saw that it was good. 22 God blessed them and said, "Be fruitful and multiply and fill the water in the seas, and let the birds multiply on the earth." 23 There was evening, and there was morning, a fifth day.

Job 39:26-30

26 "Is it by your understanding that the hawk soars, and spreads its wings toward the south? 27 Is it at your command that the eagle soars, and builds its nest on high? 28 It lives on a rock and spends the night there, on a rocky crag and a fortress. 29 From there it spots its prey, its eyes gaze intently from a distance. 30 And its young ones devour the blood, and where the dead carcasses are, there it is."

SOAP / *Job 39:26-27*
SCRIPTURE / *Write out the SOAP verses*

_____

_____

_____

_____

_____

_____

_____

_____

_____

_____

_____

_____

_____

_____

_____

_____

_____

OBSERVATION / *Write 3 - 4 observations*

_____

_____

_____

_____

_____

_____

APPLICATION / *Write down 1 - 2 applications*

_____

_____

_____

_____

_____

_____

_____

_____

_____

_____

PRAYER / *Write out a prayer over what you learned*

_____

_____

_____

_____

_____

_____

_____

_____

_____

_____

_____

_____

_____

SOAP

Job 39:26–27

Is it by your understanding that the hawk soars, and spreads its wings toward the south? Is it at your command that the eagle soars, and builds its nest on high?

INTO THE TEXT

The creation account recorded in Genesis 1 describes seven days of creation. In the first three days God created the heavens and the earth, the waters, and the land. On days four, five, and six God filled what He created on days one, two, and three. On the fifth day God created fish and birds. He filled the water with living creatures, commanding them to be fruitful and multiply. He filled the sky with birds, also commanding them to be fruitful and multiply.

God displayed His great care and provision to Job when He reminded him of the birds of prey. It is by His understanding that the hawk soars. It is by His command that an eagle flies and builds its nest. God provides food for the eagle and its young, showing her where to look for prey.

In Isaiah 40:31 God reminded the people of Judah to wait for Him, finding renewed strength in Him. They would be able to soar as if they had wings like an eagle if they would wait for Him.

In Matthew 6:25–34 Jesus told His followers not to worry. He reminded them of the birds of the air, for whom He always provides. If He has a purpose and intent in creating a bird, whom we often see as insignificant, He indeed has a purpose and intent for each of us.

Once again, God's creativity and intentionality are displayed through His creation. He created everything with purpose, even the birds. He allows us to see glimpses of His purposes for creation when He instructs us by it. And in the same way He provides for and cares for these birds, He will provide for and care for you and me.

PRAYER

Father God, You are good. Help me remember Your compassion and care for me when I see the birds. Let me be like the birds, not worrying about what I will eat, but confident You will provide what I need when I need it. Help me trust and rely on You and You alone. Amen.

1. *Why did God call all the things He created "good"? When you look at the things God created, do you see them as good?*

....

....

....

2. *How do God's questions for Job help you see creation in a new light? What surprised you about the way God described creation to Job?*

....

....

....

3. *Is God still active in creation? How so? Does God continue to mold and create the earth today the way He did in the beginning?*

....

....

....

4. *What does it mean for God to command the morning? Does it bring you comfort knowing God commands and controls the start of each new day? Why or why not?*

....

....

....

5. *God cares for and provides for each animal He created. How does this bring you assurance that God cares for and sees you?*

....

....

....

God created
humankind
in his own
image, in the
image of God
he created
them, male
and female
he created
them.

Genesis 1:27

*Write down your prayer requests
and praises for this week.*

....

....

....

....

....

....

....

....

....

....

....

....

WEEKLY CHALLENGE

*Take time this week to study what it means to be created in God's image. Is the image
of God a physical attribute or an unseen character quality? Knowing that we reflect
God's image every moment of our lives, how does this challenge you to live differently?*

....

....

....

....

....

....

....

READ

Genesis 1:24-31

24 God said, "Let the land produce living creatures according to their kinds: cattle, creeping things, and wild animals, each according to its kind." It was so. 25 God made the wild animals according to their kinds, the cattle according to their kinds, and all the creatures that creep along the ground according to their kinds. God saw that it was good.

26 Then God said, "Let us make humankind in our image, after our likeness, so they may rule over the fish of the sea and the birds of the air, over the cattle, and over all the earth, and over all the creatures that move on the earth."

27 God created humankind in his own image, in the image of God he created them, male and female he created them.

28 God blessed them and said to them, "Be fruitful and multiply! Fill the earth and subdue it! Rule over the fish of the sea and the birds of the air and every creature that moves on the ground." 29 Then God said, "I now give you every seed-bearing plant on the face of the entire earth and every tree that has fruit with seed in it. They will be yours for food. 30 And to all the animals of the earth, and to every bird of the air, and to all the creatures that move on the ground—everything that has living breath in it—I give every green plant for food." It was so.

31 God saw all that he had made—and it was very good! There was evening, and there was morning, the sixth day.

Job 39:1-12

1 "Are you acquainted with the way the mountain goats give birth? Do you watch as the wild deer give birth to their young? 2 Do you count the months they must fulfill, and do you know the time they give birth? 3 They crouch, they bear their young, they bring forth the offspring they have carried. 4 Their young grow strong, and grow up in the open; they go off, and do not return to them. 5 Who let the wild donkey go free? Who released the bonds of the donkey, 6 to whom I appointed the arid rift valley for its home, the salt wastes as its dwelling place? 7 It scorns the tumult in the town; it does not hear the shouts of a driver. 8 It ranges the hills as its pasture, and searches after every green plant. 9 Is the wild ox willing to be your servant? Will it spend the night at your feeding trough? 10 Can you bind the wild ox to a furrow with its rope, will it till the valleys, following after you? 11 Will you rely on it because its strength is great? Will you commit your labor to it? 12 Can you count on it to bring in your grain, and gather the grain to your threshing floor?

SOAP / *Genesis 1:27*
SCRIPTURE / *Write out the SOAP verses*

OBSERVATION / *Write 3 - 4 observations*

APPLICATION / *Write down 1 - 2 applications*

PRAYER / *Write out a prayer over what you learned*

SOAP

Genesis 1:27

God created humankind in his own image, in the image of God he created them, male and female he created them.

INTO THE TEXT

The sixth day of creation is both the peak and the goal of creation. God created the heavens, the earth, the sky, the sea, and the land, and then filled them with stars, birds, fish, and animals. Finally, God created humans. This was the climax of creation because humankind was like no other created thing: humankind was created in the image of God.

To be created in the image of God is far beyond our ability to comprehend. Being made in God's image does not mean we look like God. Rather, as humans, we reflect God's character and nature, not His form. We display His image when we reflect His character. We are able to create, show compassion, love, and communicate. (Sin, of course, had and continues to have an effect on our ability to reflect God's character, but as far as our reading in Genesis, sin hasn't yet entered the picture.)

Being created in the image of God means we are designed to be a reflection of who God is in the world. God has a divine purpose for creating us this way. It is our purpose to be imitators of Him. We are to be His representatives, to show His love in creation and, to those who don't know Him, His love. We are to create life like He did. We are to rule and subdue the earth. We are to display His character each and every day.

The same way God created boundaries for the rest of creation, He created boundaries for humanity. We are not God, but we have been given the great privilege of being formed in God's image. It is not a burden, but an honor to reflect Him to the world. May we live each and every day as His representatives, sharing His love with the rest of creation.

PRAYER

Lord God, it continually overwhelms me to know I am made in Your image. Help me grow in my understanding of what this means every day. Allow me to be a reflection of who You are, of Your character and Your love, to the world. Amen.

READ

Genesis 2:1-3

1 The heavens and the earth were completed with everything that was in them. 2 By the seventh day God finished the work that he had been doing, and he ceased on the seventh day all the work that he had been doing. 3 God blessed the seventh day and made it holy because on it he ceased all the work that he had been doing in creation.

Exodus 20:8-11

8 "Remember the Sabbath day to set it apart as holy. 9 For six days you may labor and do all your work, 10 but the seventh day is a Sabbath to the LORD your God; on it you shall not do any work, you, or your son, or your daughter, or your male servant, or your female servant, or your cattle, or the resident foreigner who is in your gates. 11 For in six days the LORD made the heavens and the earth and the sea and all that is in them, and he rested on the seventh day; therefore the LORD blessed the Sabbath day and set it apart as holy.

Mark 2:27

27 Then he said to them, "The Sabbath was made for people, not people for the Sabbath.

SOAP / *Exodus 20:11*
SCRIPTURE / *Write out the SOAP verses*

_____

_____

_____

_____

_____

_____

_____

_____

_____

_____

_____

_____

_____

_____

_____

_____

_____

_____

OBSERVATION / *Write 3 - 4 observations*

_____

_____

_____

_____

_____

_____

_____

APPLICATION / *Write down 1 - 2 applications*

_____
_____
_____
_____
_____
_____
_____
_____
_____
_____
_____

PRAYER / *Write out a prayer over what you learned*

_____
_____
_____
_____
_____
_____
_____
_____
_____
_____
_____
_____
_____
_____

SOAP

Exodus 20:11

For in six days the Lord made the heavens and the earth and the sea and all that is in them, and he rested on the seventh day; therefore the Lord blessed the Sabbath day and set it apart as holy.

INTO THE TEXT

God did not need to rest on the seventh day; He didn't rest because He was tired. Instead, God rested in order to establish a pattern of rest in creation. God could have made the week six days long, but instead, He added a final day: a day of rest. God built a day of rest into the pattern of time.

Years later, after God chose the nation of Israel to be His people, after God delivered them from slavery in Egypt, after God provided for them in the desert, God gave the Israelites the Ten Commandments. These commandments were meant to set God's people apart from other nations. While nine of the commands apply to every person, one of them was a new, specific command for the nation of Israel.

God commanded the Israelites to set apart the seventh day of the week as holy. The Sabbath was a symbol of God's covenant with His chosen people. While all the nations around them would continue to work, God's people stood apart when they honored the Sabbath day.

Today, we are no longer under the Old Testament law, and Sabbath is not a requirement for us to follow as Christians. However, the practice of Sabbath is something we are privileged to practice! We can rest in God's completed work, not only in creation, but in redemption from sin. Jesus has completed all the work of redeeming us. We can rest in His completed work.

Practicing Sabbath is our reminder that God's design for us is to have rest in our lives. Sabbath is a pattern we can practice now to honor God, honor the way He created the earth, and care for our bodies, families, and communities. We have the opportunity to share God's pattern of rest with the world when we take a day to cease our work and our striving and celebrate and worship Him.

PRAYER

Lord, You are good. You created a day of rest for my benefit. Help me practice Sabbath, not out of legalism, but with joy! You have completed all the work that ever needs to be done. Help me rest and be confident in Your completed work in creation and redemption. Amen.

READ

Genesis 2:4-7

4 This is the account of the heavens and the earth when they were created—when the LORD God made the earth and heavens.

5 Now no shrub of the field had yet grown on the earth, and no plant of the field had yet sprouted, for the LORD God had not caused it to rain on the earth, and there was no man to cultivate the ground. 6 Springs would well up from the earth and water the whole surface of the ground. 7 The LORD God formed the man from the soil of the ground and breathed into his nostrils the breath of life, and the man became a living being.

Psalm 8:4-6

4 Of what importance is the human race, that you should notice them? Of what importance is mankind, that you should pay attention to them? 5 You made them a little less than the heavenly beings. You crowned mankind with honor and majesty. 6 you appoint them to rule over your creation; you have placed everything under their authority,

SOAP / *Psalm 8:5-6*
SCRIPTURE / *Write out the SOAP verses*

_____

_____

_____

_____

_____

_____

_____

_____

_____

_____

_____

_____

_____

_____

_____

_____

_____

_____

OBSERVATION / *Write 3 - 4 observations*

_____

_____

_____

_____

_____

APPLICATION / *Write down 1 - 2 applications*

_____
_____
_____
_____
_____
_____
_____
_____
_____
_____
_____

PRAYER / *Write out a prayer over what you learned*

_____
_____
_____
_____
_____
_____
_____
_____
_____
_____
_____
_____
_____
_____
_____

SOAP

Psalm 8:5–6

You made them a little less than the heavenly beings. You crowned mankind with honor and majesty. You appoint them to rule over your creation; you have placed everything under their authority.

INTO THE TEXT

On the sixth day of creation God filled the land He created. He created animals, and most significantly, humans. Genesis 2 offers a detailed account, a different perspective, on the details of the creation of humanity. The detail the author of Genesis included about the creation of man and woman shows how humans are set apart from animals, how we are made in the image of God.

In Psalm 8, David reflected on the magnificence of God displayed in creation. He wondered, with the moon and stars and all their majesty, what significance do humans have? How could humans have any significance in a world with such magnificent features? Why should God notice humanity with all the splendor of creation?

God did not create humanity as an afterthought. God created us in His image, but more than that, gave us authority and honor and majesty. As image–bearers of God we are appointed to rule over creation, a little less than the heavenly beings.

In all of the magnificence of the world and the heavens, we are God's crowning creation. He chose us to bear His image. He chose us to honor His character. And He chose to redeem us when we sinned. Even in all the details and intricacies of creation, you matter to God. He cares about you, your life, and your circumstances.

PRAYER

Lord God, I am humbled and in awe of Your attention to me. You care for me. You have given me honor and majesty because I am created in Your image. May my life be an accurate reflection of Your character as I seek to display Your love and holiness to the world. Amen.

READ

Genesis 2:8-14

8 The Lord God planted an orchard in the east, in Eden; and there he placed the man he had formed. 9 The Lord God made all kinds of trees grow from the soil, every tree that was pleasing to look at and good for food. (Now the tree of life and the tree of the knowledge of good and evil were in the middle of the orchard.)

10 Now a river flows from Eden to water the orchard, and from there it divides into four headstreams. 11 The name of the first is Pishon; it runs through the entire land of Havilah, where there is gold. 12 (The gold of that land is pure; pearls and lapis lazuli are also there). 13 The name of the second river is Gihon; it runs through the entire land of Cush. 14 The name of the third river is Tigris; it runs along the east side of Assyria. The fourth river is the Euphrates.

Isaiah 58:11-12

11 The Lord will continually lead you; he will feed you even in parched regions. He will give you renewed strength, and you will be like a well-watered garden, like a spring that continually produces water. 12 Your perpetual ruins will be rebuilt; you will reestablish the ancient foundations. You will be called, 'The one who repairs broken walls, the one who makes the streets inhabitable again.'

SOAP / *Genesis 2:8-9*
SCRIPTURE / *Write out the SOAP verses*

_____

_____

_____

_____

_____

_____

_____

_____

_____

_____

_____

_____

_____

_____

_____

_____

_____

_____

_____

_____

OBSERVATION / *Write 3 - 4 observations*

_____

_____

_____

_____

_____

_____

_____

APPLICATION / *Write down 1 - 2 applications*

_____

_____

_____

_____

_____

_____

_____

_____

_____

PRAYER / *Write out a prayer over what you learned*

_____

_____

_____

_____

_____

_____

_____

_____

_____

_____

_____

_____

_____

_____

SOAP

Genesis 2:8–9

The Lord God planted an orchard in the east, in Eden; and there he placed the man he had formed. The Lord God made all kinds of trees grow from the soil, every tree that was pleasing to look at and good for food. (Now the tree of life and the tree of the knowledge of good and evil were in the middle of the orchard.)

INTO THE TEXT

After God created the man, He provided a place for him to live. This was no ordinary place. It was paradise. God created a place for the man to live that was full of blessing.

God planted all kinds of trees, both for beauty and for sustenance. God planted the orchard among four rivers, providing water and continued life for both the man and all God had planted. Everything he needed was there for him.

The location of the orchard is described in detail. It may seem like unimportant or unnecessary details to us today, but the detail was not lost on the original audience. This orchard was planted in an incredibly fertile area of the Middle East, later known as "The Fertile Crescent." God not only provided for the man by giving him a home with enough food and water to survive, but He gave the man an abundance of resources in order for him to thrive and multiply.

Before sin entered the world, God provided for the man in the orchard. And, as we'll see, God continued to provide even after the man and woman sinned. Isaiah's words in chapter 58 show how God continued to lead and provide for His people even when they sinned and rebelled against Him.

Our God is a good God. He provides for His people no matter the circumstance. He provided for the man in the orchard and He provided for the remnant of Judah. He provides for you and for me each and every day. May we look for not only His provision, but for His continual presence and grace in our lives.

PRAYER

Lord God, You provide exactly what I need. Today, help me remember and bring to mind all the ways You provide for me and bless me. I praise You for Your care for me. Amen.

READ

Genesis 2:15-17

15 The LORD God took the man and placed him in the orchard in Eden to care for it and to maintain it. 16 Then the LORD God commanded the man, "You may freely eat fruit from every tree of the orchard, 17 but you must not eat from the tree of the knowledge of good and evil, for when you eat from it you will surely die."

Psalm 19:7-11

7 The law of the LORD is perfect and preserves one's life. The rules set down by the LORD are reliable and impart wisdom to the inexperienced. 8 The LORD's precepts are fair and make one joyful. The LORD's commands are pure and give insight for life. 9 The commands to fear the LORD are right and endure forever. The judgments given by the LORD are trustworthy and absolutely just. 10 They are of greater value than gold, than even a great amount of pure gold; they bring greater delight than honey, than even the sweetest honey from a honeycomb. 11 Yes, your servant finds moral guidance there; those who obey them receive a rich reward.

SOAP

SOAP / *Psalm 19:7-8*
SCRIPTURE / *Write out the SOAP verses*

_____

_____

_____

_____

_____

_____

_____

_____

_____

_____

_____

_____

_____

_____

_____

_____

_____

_____

OBSERVATION / *Write 3 - 4 observations*

_____

_____

_____

_____

_____

_____

_____

APPLICATION / *Write down 1 - 2 applications*

PRAYER / *Write out a prayer over what you learned*

SOAP

Psalm 19:7–8

The law of the Lord is perfect and preserves one's life. The rules set down by the Lord are reliable and impart wisdom to the inexperienced. The Lord's precepts are fair and make one joyful. The Lord's commands are pure and give insight for life.

INTO THE TEXT

When God created the orchard He planted two important trees: the tree of life and the Tree of Knowledge of Good and Evil. (This is the first reference the writer of Genesis made to good and evil.) The placement of the trees in the orchard set the stage for what was to come, the continual struggle and choice for the man and his offspring between good and evil.

When God placed the man in the orchard to care for and maintain it, He gave the man specific instructions. He commanded the man not to eat from the Tree of Knowledge of Good and Evil. God knew that if the man were to eat from this tree he would die. The idea of death introduced in this command was more than a physical death, though that was included as well. The death that would occur for the man if he ate from the tree was a separation or alienation from God, causing a dramatic change in his relationship with his Creator.

The command to not eat from the Tree of Knowledge of Good and Evil is the first command God gave to humanity. In the same way all aspects of creation were designed with a purpose and intent, God had an intention with His command for the man. God knew what would happen if the man were to eat from the tree, so God told the man not to eat from it.

God's first command to the man was good. It was meant to preserve the man's life. All of God's commands are meant to do this. All of God's commands preserve our lives, give us wisdom, and bring joy. They have great value and purpose, and in following them we find guidance and blessing. While it is easy to see how this first command of God's was right, it is not always as easy to see how all of God's commands are right. When we keep our hearts fixed on Him we find wisdom in His commands and joy and life in keeping them.

PRAYER

Father God, Your law is perfect. Your law preserves my life. I can rely on Your instruction and gain wisdom from Your commands. I believe Your words are of greater value than gold. Help me desire Your way over mine. Amen.

1. *What does it mean to be made in the image of God?*

....

....

....

2. *What makes the Sabbath day holy? Should we still observe the Sabbath today, even though we are not under the Old Testament law?*

....

....

....

3. *What does it mean that humans have dominion over the earth? How should we treat the earth based on this truth?*

....

....

....

4. *What new things did you learn about the orchard God planted? What stands out to you as surprising or confusing in God's creation of the orchard?*

....

....

....

5. *Why can we trust God's law? Are there any laws or commands of God that don't seem right to you? What do you do when you have questions about what God says?*

....

....

....

Now the law came in so that the transgression may increase, but where sin increased, grace multiplied all the more, so that just as sin reigned in death, so also grace will reign through righteousness to eternal life through Jesus Christ our Lord.

Romans 5:20-21

*Write down your prayer requests
and praises for this week.*

....
....
....
....
....
....
....
....
....
....
....
....

WEEKLY CHALLENGE

*The serpent took something God said to Eve and twisted it. He made her question
God's commands. What can we do to combat the lies of the enemy? He often whispers
"half-truths" to us, causing us to question God's promises or commands. What can
we do to combat these attacks and remain steadfast in our faith and convictions?*

....
....
....
....
....
....
....

READ

Genesis 2:18-25

18 The Lord God said, "It is not good for the man to be alone. I will make a companion for him who corresponds to him." 19 The Lord God formed out of the ground every living animal of the field and every bird of the air. He brought them to the man to see what he would name them, and whatever the man called each living creature, that was its name. 20 So the man named all the animals, the birds of the air, and the living creatures of the field, but for Adam no companion who corresponded to him was found. 21 So the Lord God caused the man to fall into a deep sleep, and while he was asleep, he took part of the man's side and closed up the place with flesh. 22 Then the Lord God made a woman from the part he had taken out of the man, and he brought her to the man. 23 Then the man said,

"This one at last is bone of my bones and flesh of my flesh; this one will be called 'woman,' for she was taken out of man."

24 That is why a man leaves his father and mother and unites with his wife, and they become one family. 25 The man and his wife were both naked, but they were not ashamed.

Matthew 19:4-6

4 He answered, "Have you not read that from the beginning the Creator **made them male and female**, 5 and said, '**For this reason a man will leave his father and mother and will be united with his wife, and the two will become one flesh**'? 6 So they are no longer two, but one flesh. Therefore what God has joined together, let no one separate."

SOAP / *Matthew 19:4-6*
SCRIPTURE / *Write out the SOAP verses*

_____

_____

_____

_____

_____

_____

_____

_____

_____

_____

_____

_____

_____

_____

_____

_____

_____

_____

OBSERVATION / *Write 3 - 4 observations*

_____

_____

_____

_____

_____

_____

APPLICATION / *Write down 1 - 2 applications*

_____

_____

_____

_____

_____

_____

_____

_____

_____

_____

PRAYER / *Write out a prayer over what you learned*

_____

_____

_____

_____

_____

_____

_____

_____

_____

_____

_____

_____

_____

_____

_____

SOAP

Matthew 19:4–6

He answered, "Have you not read that from the beginning the Creator **made them male and female**, *and said,* '**For this reason a man will leave his father and mother and will be united with his wife, and the two will become one flesh**'? *So they are no longer two, but one flesh. Therefore what God has joined together, let no one separate."*

INTO THE TEXT

It was not good for the man to be alone. This is the only aspect of creation to this point that God said was not good. While the man was alone, there is not an indication he was lonely. What God called "not good" was the absence of community for the man. The man was alone because there was no one like him with whom he could share all God had planned for humanity. He was not able to fulfill God's purpose for humanity to "be fruitful and multiply" by himself.

God created the woman to be a companion to the man. The Hebrew word used to describe the woman as a companion is the word '*ezer*. Most of the other uses of '*ezer* in the Old Testament are used to describe God. This word has no sense of inferiority or subordination but rather describes an indispensable companion, one who does for us what we cannot do for ourselves.

When the Pharisees questioned Jesus about divorce, He answered them by explaining the purpose of a relationship between a man and a woman. The two are to be joined together, becoming one. In marriage, a man and woman become one, both becoming indispensable companions to one another. When the author of Genesis described the first man and woman he described their marriage relationship. The community they experienced was through marriage.

Man and woman were designed to live in community. Whether married or single, we cannot live alone. We need community and others around us. God designed us for community and we are not complete without it. As followers of Christ we cannot be alone. We need community with one another to encourage each other in our walk with Christ.

PRAYER

God, thank You for creating me for community. I am blessed by those around me. Help me to be a blessing to others. Help me grow in my understanding of community and the need I have for it. Guard and build my community today as You teach me more of what it means to not be alone. Amen.

READ

Genesis 3:1-7

1 Now the serpent was shrewder than any of the wild animals that the LORD God had made. He said to the woman, "Is it really true that God said, 'You must not eat from any tree of the orchard'?" 2 The woman said to the serpent, "We may eat of the fruit from the trees of the orchard; 3 but concerning the fruit of the tree that is in the middle of the orchard God said, 'You must not eat from it, and you must not touch it, or else you will die.'" 4 The serpent said to the woman, "Surely you will not die, 5 for God knows that when you eat from it your eyes will open and you will be like God, knowing good and evil."

6 When the woman saw that the tree produced fruit that was good for food, was attractive to the eye, and was desirable for making one wise, she took some of its fruit and ate it. She also gave some of it to her husband who was with her, and he ate it. 7 Then the eyes of both of them opened, and they knew they were naked; so they sewed fig leaves together and made coverings for themselves.

1 Peter 5:8-9

8 Be sober and alert. Your enemy the devil, like a roaring lion, is on the prowl looking for someone to devour. 9 Resist him, strong in your faith, because you know that your brothers and sisters throughout the world are enduring the same kinds of suffering.

SOAP / *1 Peter 5:8-9*
SCRIPTURE / *Write out the SOAP verses*

OBSERVATION / *Write 3 - 4 observations*

APPLICATION / *Write down 1 - 2 applications*

_____
_____
_____
_____
_____
_____
_____
_____
_____
_____
_____

PRAYER / *Write out a prayer over what you learned*

_____
_____
_____
_____
_____
_____
_____
_____
_____
_____
_____
_____
_____
_____
_____

SOAP

1 Peter 5:8–9

Be sober and alert. Your enemy the devil, like a roaring lion, is on the prowl looking for someone to devour. Resist him, strong in your faith, because you know that your brothers and sisters throughout the world are enduring the same kinds of suffering.

INTO THE TEXT

The serpent knew how to trick the woman. He knew how to twist the words and commands of God to get her to believe God was holding out on her. What he said was partially true, but not completely. He framed God's words in such a way to cause the woman to believe God was keeping something good from her.

The woman also was a bit unsure of what God had said. She told the serpent God had said they could not eat from the tree or touch the tree. God only said they could not eat from the tree. This additional command to not touch the tree did not come from God. Whether the man said this to the woman or they decided on it together, it was not from God.

The serpent continued to lie to the woman. He told her she would receive something good—wisdom—not death like God had said. He was on the prowl, looking to devour the woman. The woman and the man failed to follow God's commands and took the serpent's tempting offer.

When we face temptation to sin we often face a similar set of circumstances. The enemy may try to convince us of something that is partially true, or has elements of truth in it. He tries to trick and trap us at every turn, like a lion searching for prey. But there is hope! We are not to fall prey to his schemes. With God's help we can stand against temptation. As we study and memorize God's Word we become armed with truth. When we know the truth, when we are sure of exactly what God says, without adding to it or taking away from it, we are best armed to face the attacks of the enemy.

PRAYER

Lord Jesus, give me wisdom to know what is true and what is not true. Help me stand firm against the schemes of the enemy, aware he is always out to trap me. I desire to honor Your Word and follow You. Amen.

READ

Genesis 3:8-19

8 Then the man and his wife heard the sound of the LORD God moving about in the orchard at the breezy time of the day, and they hid from the LORD God among the trees of the orchard. 9 But the LORD God called to the man and said to him, "Where are you?" 10 The man replied, "I heard you moving about in the orchard, and I was afraid because I was naked, so I hid." 11 And the LORD God said, "Who told you that you were naked? Did you eat from the tree that I commanded you not to eat from?" 12 The man said, "The woman whom you gave me, she gave me some fruit from the tree and I ate it." 13 So the LORD God said to the woman, "What is this you have done?" And the woman replied, "The serpent tricked me, and I ate."

14 The LORD God said to the serpent, "Because you have done this, cursed are you above all the cattle and all the living creatures of the field! On your belly you will crawl and dust you will eat all the days of your life. 15 And I will put hostility between you and the woman and between your offspring and her offspring; he will strike your head, and you will strike his heel." 16 To the woman he said, "I will greatly increase your labor pains; with pain you will give birth to children. You will want to control your husband, but he will dominate you." 17 But to Adam he said, "Because you obeyed your wife and ate from the tree about which I commanded you, 'You must not eat from it,' the ground is cursed because of you; in painful toil you will eat of it all the days of your life. 18 It will produce thorns and thistles for you, but you will eat the grain of the field. 19 By the sweat of your brow you will eat food until you return to the ground, for out of it you were taken; for you are dust, and to dust you will return."

Romans 5:20-21

20 Now the law came in so that the transgression may increase, but where sin increased, grace multiplied all the more, 21 so that just as sin reigned in death, so also grace will reign through righteousness to eternal life through Jesus Christ our LORD.

SOAP / *Romans 5:20-21*
SCRIPTURE / *Write out the SOAP verses*

_____

_____

_____

_____

_____

_____

_____

_____

_____

_____

_____

_____

_____

_____

_____

_____

_____

_____

OBSERVATION / *Write 3 - 4 observations*

_____

_____

_____

_____

_____

_____

APPLICATION / *Write down 1 - 2 applications*

_____

_____

_____

_____

_____

_____

_____

_____

_____

_____

PRAYER / *Write out a prayer over what you learned*

_____

_____

_____

_____

_____

_____

_____

_____

_____

_____

_____

_____

_____

_____

SOAP

Romans 5:20–21

Now the law came in so that the transgression may increase, but where sin increased, grace multiplied all the more, so that just as sin reigned in death, so also grace will reign through righteousness to eternal life through Jesus Christ our Lord.

INTO THE TEXT

The man and the woman ate from the tree in the orchard. They were separated from God because of their sin. They were immediately aware of their nakedness and hid in shame. The relationship between God and humanity changed. The man and the woman could no longer be in the presence of God because they had sinned.

While the man and woman had both sinned, each tried to shift blame to another. The man tried to shift blame to the woman. The woman tried to shift blame to the serpent. The reality was, they both had sinned. They were both equally responsible for their actions and they both received a punishment.

Yet even when explaining the punishment they would receive, God promised to redeem the man and the woman to a right relationship with Him. God promised that even though the serpent and his offspring may try to attack the woman and her offspring, he would fail. God promised that the offspring of the woman (who ultimately is Jesus) would crush the head of the serpent.

Even in the midst of punishment, God promised redemption. With every command God gave to His people, their sin increased. Yet as sin increased, grace multiplied all the more. God planned redemption even before our transgression. Grace reigns in the midst of all our faults, even those that seem beyond redemption. Grace reigns through the righteousness of Jesus Christ. God orchestrated the redemption of humanity even before we began to sin. God showers us with His grace, even now, no matter our sin. Praise Him!

PRAYER

God, You alone are good. I am beyond humbled that You would plan redemption for me even before I sinned. You shower me with Your grace each and every day. You alone are worthy of praise. Let my life be a reflection of Your grace and redemption. Amen.

READ

Genesis 3:20-24

20 The man named his wife Eve, because she was the mother of all the living. 21 The LORD God made garments from skin for Adam and his wife, and clothed them. 22 And the LORD God said, "Now that the man has become like one of us, knowing good and evil, he must not be allowed to stretch out his hand and take also from the tree of life and eat, and live forever." 23 So the LORD God expelled him from the orchard in Eden to cultivate the ground from which he had been taken. 24 When he drove the man out, he placed on the eastern side of the orchard in Eden angelic sentries who used the flame of a whirling sword to guard the way to the tree of life.

Ephesians 2:4-10

4 But God, being rich in mercy, because of his great love with which he loved us, 5 even though we were dead in offenses, made us alive together with Christ—by grace you are saved!— 6 and he raised us up together with him and seated us together with him in the heavenly realms in Christ Jesus, 7 to demonstrate in the coming ages the surpassing wealth of his grace in kindness toward us in Christ Jesus. 8 For by grace you are saved through faith, and this is not from yourselves, it is the gift of God; 9 it is not from works, so that no one can boast. 10 For we are his creative work, having been created in Christ Jesus for good works that God prepared beforehand so we can do them.

SOAP / *Ephesians 2:8*
SCRIPTURE / *Write out the SOAP verses*

_____

_____

_____

_____

_____

_____

_____

_____

_____

_____

_____

_____

_____

_____

_____

_____

_____

_____

_____

OBSERVATION / *Write 3 - 4 observations*

_____

_____

_____

_____

_____

_____

APPLICATION / *Write down 1 - 2 applications*

_____

_____

_____

_____

_____

_____

_____

_____

_____

_____

PRAYER / *Write out a prayer over what you learned*

_____

_____

_____

_____

_____

_____

_____

_____

_____

_____

_____

_____

_____

_____

SOAP

Ephesians 2:8

For by grace you are saved through faith, and this is not from yourselves, it is the gift of God.

INTO THE TEXT

Adam and Eve ate the fruit from the Tree of Knowledge of Good and Evil. God said if they did this, they would die. Even though they did not physically die at that moment, they were dead in a spiritual sense. They would die because of their sin. They were dead, separated from God because of their sin.

But Adam and Eve's God, our God, is rich in mercy. He loves us, even though we are dead in our sin. God loved and cared for Adam and Eve. He covered the disgrace of their sin with clothing. These coverings were made from skin, meaning an animal had to die as a sacrifice in order to cover them.

God sent Adam and Eve out from the orchard. Sending them out of the orchard may have seemed like the worst option, but it was God's provision and care. Instead of allowing them to be tempted and possibly eat from the tree of life, God sent them out of the orchard.

We too are separated from God. We are dead in our sins, just like Adam and Eve. We need a covering, a sacrifice for our sins. Jesus Christ is that covering. Jesus Christ sacrificed Himself so we could be spared from the punishment of sin.

We are saved by the grace of God. In the same way God, in His great grace, provided coverings for Adam and Eve and sent them out from the orchard, God provided a covering for us in Jesus. His sacrifice is grace alone. Through faith, we can accept God's gift of grace, Jesus Christ. When we place our faith in Him we accept the provision He has given us, for our lives and for our salvation.

PRAYER

Lord Jesus, You alone are the covering I need. You have saved me by Your grace alone. There is nothing I have done to earn my salvation. I have placed my faith in You for my salvation. Help me continue to place my faith in You every day. You alone are my covering and my provision. Amen.

READ

Genesis 4:1-16

1 Now the man was intimate with his wife Eve, and she became pregnant and gave birth to Cain. Then she said, "I have created a man just as the LORD did!" 2 Then she gave birth to his brother Abel. Abel took care of the flocks, while Cain cultivated the ground.

3 At the designated time Cain brought some of the fruit of the ground for an offering to the LORD. 4 But Abel brought some of the firstborn of his flock— even the fattest of them. And the LORD was pleased with Abel and his offering, 5 but with Cain and his offering he was not pleased. So Cain became very angry, and his expression was downcast.

6 Then the LORD said to Cain, "Why are you angry, and why is your expression downcast? 7 Is it not true that if you do what is right, you will be fine? But if you do not do what is right, sin is crouching at the door. It desires to dominate you, but you must subdue it."

8 Cain said to his brother Abel, "Let's go out to the field." While they were in the field, Cain attacked his brother Abel and killed him.

9 Then the LORD said to Cain, "Where is your brother Abel?" And he replied, "I don't know! Am I my brother's guardian?" 10 But the LORD said, "What have you done? The voice of your brother's blood is crying out to me from the ground! 11 So now you are banished from the ground, which has opened its mouth to receive your brother's blood from your hand. 12 When you try to cultivate the ground it will no longer yield its best for you. You will be a homeless wanderer on the earth."

13 Then Cain said to the LORD, "My punishment is too great to endure! 14 Look, you are driving me off the land today, and I must hide from your presence. I will be a homeless wanderer on the earth; whoever finds me will kill me!" 15 But the LORD said to him, "All right then, if anyone kills Cain, Cain will be avenged seven times as much." Then the LORD put a special mark on Cain so that no one who found him would strike him down. 16 So Cain went out from the presence of the LORD and lived in the land of Nod, east of Eden.

Psalm 51:17

17 The sacrifice God desires is a humble spirit— O God, a humble and repentant heart you will not reject.

Hosea 6:6

6 For I delight in faithfulness, not simply in sacrifice; I delight in acknowledging God, not simply in whole burnt offerings.

SOAP / *Hosea 6:6*
SCRIPTURE / *Write out the SOAP verses*

_____

_____

_____

_____

_____

_____

_____

_____

_____

_____

_____

_____

_____

_____

_____

_____

_____

OBSERVATION / *Write 3 - 4 observations*

_____

_____

_____

_____

_____

_____

APPLICATION / *Write down 1 - 2 applications*

_____
_____
_____
_____
_____
_____
_____
_____
_____
_____
_____
_____
_____

PRAYER / *Write out a prayer over what you learned*

_____
_____
_____
_____
_____
_____
_____
_____
_____
_____
_____
_____
_____
_____
_____
_____
_____

SOAP

Hosea 6:6

For I delight in faithfulness, not simply in sacrifice; I delight in acknowledging God, not simply in whole burnt offerings.

INTO THE TEXT

Cain brought a sacrifice to God from his crops. Abel went out of his way to please God by bringing a sacrifice from the best of his flock. While we are not certain of Cain's exact motivation for his sacrifice, it is clear that whatever it was, it did not please God. God accepted Abel's sacrifice but rejected Cain's.

God warned Cain to check his heart and his motives, for if he continued to not do what was right, sin would dominate him. Cain wanted to give in to his sin. Instead of heading God's warning, he went out and murdered his brother.

God's desire was not for Cain to bring the exact same sacrifice as Abel had brought. Even though God had not (as far as we know) yet spelled out the stipulations and requirements for sacrifices, like He did in Leviticus for the Israelites, He did desire that the hearts of His people be turned to Him in worship.

When we stand before God in worship, He is not criticizing us for the exact details of what we lay before Him. Instead, He desires that we are faithful to Him, humble toward Him, and repentant to Him. God desires our hearts, not just our actions. Our lives are to be a sacrifice to Him. When our hearts are right with God we will go out of our way to please Him by offering our best. Ritual is not what God is after. He wants our hearts to be longing for Him, humbled by Him daily, and in awe of all He has given us.

PRAYER

Father God, guard my life. Help me live my life as a living sacrifice to You, going out of my way to please You and bring my best to You. I long to bring an offering like Abel. Help me stay alert to the sin crouching at my door and remain humble and repentant to You. Amen.

1. *How are we, as Christians, to honor the covenant of marriage, whether we are married or single?*

....

....

....

2. *What are three practical things you can do today to resist the enemy?*

....

....

....

3. *What does it mean that grace increased when sin increased? Why would God continue to show us grace when we continually sin against Him?*

....

....

....

4. *What encouragement do you find in Ephesians 2:8? What does it mean that salvation is not from ourselves but instead is a gift of God?*

....

....

....

5. *How do we test our motives when we are tempted to go through the motions in our walk with God? What can we do to combat the temptation to "check the box" when our hearts are far from God?*

....

....

....

For all have
sinned and fall
short of the glory
of God. But
they are justified
freely by his grace
through the
redemption that
is in Christ Jesus.

Romans 3:23-24

*Write down your prayer requests
and praises for this week.*

....

....

....

....

....

....

....

....

....

....

....

....

....

WEEKLY CHALLENGE

*We are commanded to praise the Lord with all we have. This week, spend intentional
time praising God each day. Praise Him for His character, not just what He does for
you or has given you. How can you honor Him this week?*

....

....

....

....

....

....

....

....

READ

Genesis 4:17-26

17 Cain was intimate with his wife, and she became pregnant and gave birth to Enoch. Cain was building a city, and he named the city after his son Enoch. 18 To Enoch was born Irad, and Irad was the father of Mehujael. Mehujael was the father of Methushael, and Methushael was the father of Lamech.

19 Lamech took two wives for himself; the name of the first was Adah, and the name of the second was Zillah. 20 Adah gave birth to Jabal; he was the first of those who live in tents and keep livestock. 21 The name of his brother was Jubal; he was the first of all who play the harp and the flute. 22 Now Zillah also gave birth to Tubal-Cain, who heated metal and shaped all kinds of tools made of bronze and iron. The sister of Tubal-Cain was Naamah.

23 Lamech said to his wives, "Adah and Zillah, listen to me! You wives of Lamech, hear my words! I have killed a man for wounding me, a young man for hurting me. 24 If Cain is to be avenged seven times as much, then Lamech seventy-seven times!"

25 And Adam was intimate with his wife again, and she gave birth to a son. She named him Seth, saying, "God has given me another child in place of Abel because Cain killed him." 26 And a son was also born to Seth, whom he named Enosh. At that time people began to worship the LORD.

Psalm 150

1 Praise the LORD! Praise God in his sanctuary; praise him in the sky, which testifies to his strength! 2 Praise him for his mighty acts; praise him for his surpassing greatness! 3 Praise him with the blast of the horn; praise him with the lyre and the harp! 4 Praise him with the tambourine and with dancing; praise him with stringed instruments and the flute! 5 Praise him with loud cymbals; praise him with clanging cymbals! 6 Let everything that has breath praise the LORD! Praise the LORD!

SOAP / *Psalm 150:1-6*
SCRIPTURE / *Write out the SOAP verses*

_____

_____

_____

_____

_____

_____

_____

_____

_____

_____

_____

_____

_____

_____

_____

_____

_____

_____

_____

_____

OBSERVATION / *Write 3 - 4 observations*

_____

_____

_____

_____

_____

_____

_____

APPLICATION / *Write down 1 - 2 applications*

_____

_____

_____

_____

_____

_____

_____

_____

_____

_____

PRAYER / *Write out a prayer over what you learned*

_____

_____

_____

_____

_____

_____

_____

_____

_____

_____

_____

_____

_____

_____

SOAP

Psalm 150:1–6

Praise the Lord! Praise God in his sanctuary; praise him in the sky, which testifies to his strength! Praise him for his mighty acts; praise him for his surpassing greatness! Praise him with the blast of the horn; praise him with the lyre and the harp! Praise him with the tambourine and with dancing; praise him with stringed instruments and the flute! Praise him with loud cymbals; praise him with clanging cymbals! Let everything that has breath praise the Lord! Praise the Lord!

INTO THE TEXT

After telling the story of Cain and Abel, the author of Genesis shifts to a few chapters of family histories. While these genealogies include only a handful of details about those mentioned, the way in which they are written and structured displays important truths and principles for life with God.

The line of Cain took after their patriarch. Cain's sinful choices affected his descendants for many generations. They showed disregard for God as they took multiple wives, sought success and fame, and even murdered others. Cain's genealogy also shows the first cities and cultures, including the first musicians and craftsmen.

Seth's line shows a direct contrast to Cain's. As we will see in later readings, many of Seth's descendants feared and worshiped God. We also see the first reference that people called on God's name and worshiped Him.

No matter the culture around us, no matter our circumstances, our successes, our status, or our talents, the worship of God is what brings life. While Cain's descendants did many great things, they were far from God. They sought their own gain instead of making God's name great. Without preserving the worship and knowledge of God in our lives, our families, our cultures, and our nations, we too will fall into sin and destruction as Cain's descendants did. Instead, may we be people who call on the name of the Lord, who worship His name and make Him known wherever we are.

Let everything that has breath praise the Lord!

PRAYER

Lord God, You alone deserve to be worshiped. You alone are worthy of praise. Your surpassing greatness is more than anything on earth. Help me praise You no matter my circumstances. Help me turn from sin and worship You. Amen.

READ

Genesis 5:1-32

1 This is the record of the family line of Adam.

When God created humankind, he made them in the likeness of God. 2 He created them male and female; when they were created, he blessed them and named them "humankind."

3 When Adam had lived 130 years he fathered a son in his own likeness, according to his image, and he named him Seth. 4 The length of time Adam lived after he became the father of Seth was 800 years; during this time he had other sons and daughters. 5 The entire lifetime of Adam was 930 years, and then he died.

6 When Seth had lived 105 years, he became the father of Enosh. 7 Seth lived 807 years after he became the father of Enosh, and he had other sons and daughters. 8 The entire lifetime of Seth was 912 years, and then he died.

9 When Enosh had lived 90 years, he became the father of Kenan. 10 Enosh lived 815 years after he became the father of Kenan, and he had other sons and daughters. 11 The entire lifetime of Enosh was 905 years, and then he died.

12 When Kenan had lived 70 years, he became the father of Mahalalel. 13 Kenan lived 840 years after he became the father of Mahalalel, and he had other sons and daughters. 14 The entire lifetime of Kenan was 910 years, and then he died.

15 When Mahalalel had lived 65 years, he became the father of Jared. 16 Mahalalel lived 830 years after he became the father of Jared, and he had other sons and daughters. 17 The entire lifetime of Mahalalel was 895 years, and then he died.

18 When Jared had lived 162 years, he became the father of Enoch. 19 Jared lived 800 years after he became the father of Enoch, and he had other sons and daughters. 20 The entire lifetime of Jared was 962 years, and then he died.

Genesis 5:1-32 (continued)

21 When Enoch had lived 65 years, he became the father of Methuselah. 22 After he became the father of Methuselah, Enoch walked with God for 300 years, and he had other sons and daughters. 23 The entire lifetime of Enoch was 365 years. 24 Enoch walked with God, and then he disappeared because God took him away.

25 When Methuselah had lived 187 years, he became the father of Lamech. 26 Methuselah lived 782 years after he became the father of Lamech, and he had other sons and daughters. 27 The entire lifetime of Methuselah was 969 years, and then he died.

28 When Lamech had lived 182 years, he had a son. 29 He named him Noah, saying, "This one will bring us comfort from our labor and from the painful toil of our hands because of the ground that the LORD has cursed." 30 Lamech lived 595 years after he became the father of Noah, and he had other sons and daughters. 31 The entire lifetime of Lamech was 777 years, and then he died.

32 After Noah was 500 years old, he became the father of Shem, Ham, and Japheth.

Psalm 39:4-6

4 "O LORD, help me understand my mortality and the brevity of life. Let me realize how quickly my life will pass. 5 Look, you make my days short-lived, and my life span is nothing from your perspective. Surely all people, even those who seem secure, are nothing but vapor. (Selah) 6 Surely people go through life as mere ghosts. Surely they accumulate worthless wealth without knowing who will eventually haul it away."

"Neither can I call myself anything else than what I am, a Christian."

Perpetua

SOAP / *Genesis 5:24*
SCRIPTURE / *Write out the SOAP verses*

_____

_____

_____

_____

_____

_____

_____

_____

_____

_____

_____

_____

_____

_____

_____

_____

_____

_____

_____

OBSERVATION / *Write 3 - 4 observations*

_____

_____

_____

_____

_____

_____

APPLICATION / *Write down 1 - 2 applications*

_____

_____

_____

_____

_____

_____

_____

_____

_____

_____

PRAYER / *Write out a prayer over what you learned*

_____

_____

_____

_____

_____

_____

_____

_____

_____

_____

_____

_____

_____

_____

SOAP

Genesis 5:24

Enoch walked with God, and then he disappeared because God took him away.

INTO THE TEXT

The family line of Adam, specifically through Seth, displays the realities of life and death. Among all the names on this list, Enoch is the only one whose relationship with God is mentioned. Not much is said, only that Enoch walked with God. It is not specified for how long or in what ways Enoch walked with God. But Enoch's life looked drastically different than anyone else on earth. Enoch did not die, but instead, God took him away.

Enoch's life stands in contrast with the others mentioned in Seth's line and those mentioned in Cain's line. Unlike Cain's descendants, Enoch walked with God. Instead of pursuing wealth and status like Cain's descendants, he sought the Lord. He also stands out among Seth's descendants because of his commitment to God.

Genesis 5 brings us face to face with mortality. Even though the people mentioned in this section lived much longer than we can imagine living today, they still died. No matter how long and full their lives were, they still faced death. Except one. Enoch's life stands apart because of his walk with God. Through Enoch's example, the author of Genesis tells us that everlasting life is only found in a relationship with God.

When we have a fuller understanding of our mortality, we are better able to see what does and doesn't matter in life. God's Word and the souls of people are the only things that will last into eternity. Our days are not long, but they can be marked by fullness when we walk with and worship God.

PRAYER

Lord, help me understand my mortality. My life is only a blink from Your perspective. Help me remain faithful to You as I live my life. I want to walk with You the way Enoch did. Show me what it means to have a heart and life committed to You each day. Amen.

READ

Genesis 6:1-8

1 When humankind began to multiply on the face of the earth, and daughters were born to them, 2 the sons of God saw that the daughters of humankind were beautiful. Thus they took wives for themselves from any they chose. 3 So the Lord said, "My Spirit will not remain in humankind indefinitely, since they are mortal. They will remain for 120 more years."

4 The Nephilim were on the earth in those days (and also after this) when the sons of God would sleep with the daughters of humankind, who gave birth to their children. They were the mighty heroes of old, the famous men.

5 But the Lord saw that the wickedness of humankind had become great on the earth. Every inclination of the thoughts of their minds was only evil all the time. 6 The Lord regretted that he had made humankind on the earth, and he was highly offended. 7 So the Lord said, "I will wipe humankind, whom I have created, from the face of the earth—everything from humankind to animals, including creatures that move on the ground and birds of the air, for I regret that I have made them."

8 But Noah found favor in the sight of the Lord.

Romans 3:21-26

21 But now apart from the law the righteousness of God (although it is attested by the law and the prophets) has been disclosed— 22 namely, the righteousness of God through the faithfulness of Jesus Christ for all who believe. For there is no distinction, 23 for all have sinned and fall short of the glory of God. 24 But they are justified freely by his grace through the redemption that is in Christ Jesus. 25 God publicly displayed him at his death as the mercy seat accessible through faith. This was to demonstrate his righteousness, because God in his forbearance had passed over the sins previously committed. 26 This was also to demonstrate his righteousness in the present time, so that he would be just and the justifier of the one who lives because of Jesus' faithfulness.

SOAP / *Romans 3:23-24*
SCRIPTURE / *Write out the SOAP verses*

_____

_____

_____

_____

_____

_____

_____

_____

_____

_____

_____

_____

_____

_____

_____

_____

_____

_____

_____

OBSERVATION / *Write 3 - 4 observations*

_____

_____

_____

_____

_____

_____

_____

APPLICATION / *Write down 1 - 2 applications*

_____

_____

_____

_____

_____

_____

_____

_____

_____

_____

PRAYER / *Write out a prayer over what you learned*

_____

_____

_____

_____

_____

_____

_____

_____

_____

_____

_____

_____

_____

_____

_____

_____

SOAP

Romans 3:23–24

For all have sinned and fall short of the glory of God. But they are justified freely by his grace through the redemption that is in Christ Jesus.

INTO THE TEXT

The meaning of Genesis 6:1-4 is debated by evangelical scholars. One possible interpretation says the sons of God were the line of Seth and the daughters of men were descendants of Cain. Cain's wicked descendants enticed Seth's descendants, who were committed to God, to sin. Another interpretation believes the sons of God were fallen angels who left their position in heaven and the daughters of men were women whom they slept with.

While we do not know definitively the actual meaning of these verses, the hearts of people had clearly become wicked. Wickedness became great and every thought from every mind was evil. The Lord was offended and even regretted making humans.

But grace. Even in the midst of such wickedness, even in the midst of a horrible offense against Him, God provided redemption. Noah found favor in the eyes of God, not by anything he had done, but by God's grace alone. God extended grace to humanity, allowing the race to continue through Noah's family.

Humanity is still wicked and sinful. We have been born into sinful existence, always turning away from God. We have all fallen short of His glory and righteousness. God justifies us anyway. God is rich in mercy, full of love, and great in compassion. He overwhelms us with His grace by sending a redeemer, Jesus Christ. We have all sinned and fallen short of His standard, but by His grace alone, we are justified and redeemed.

PRAYER

Lord God, I am in awe of Your grace. I am undeserving of Your incredible love and compassion. I do not deserve Your grace and Your redemption. I praise You for Your kindness and forgiveness to me. In Jesus' name, amen.

READ

Genesis 6:9-22

9 This is the account of Noah.

Noah was a godly man; he was blameless among his contemporaries. He walked with God. 10 Noah had three sons: Shem, Ham, and Japheth.

11 The earth was ruined in the sight of God; the earth was filled with violence. 12 God saw the earth, and indeed it was ruined, for all living creatures on the earth were sinful. 13 So God said to Noah, "I have decided that all living creatures must die, for the earth is filled with violence because of them. Now I am about to destroy them and the earth. 14 Make for yourself an ark of cypress wood. Make rooms in the ark, and cover it with pitch inside and out. 15 This is how you should make it: The ark is to be 450 feet long, 75 feet wide, and 45 feet high. 16 Make a roof for the ark and finish it, leaving 18 inches from the top. Put a door in the side of the ark, and make lower, middle, and upper decks. 17 I am about to bring floodwaters on the earth to destroy from under the sky all the living creatures that have the breath of life in them. Everything that is on the earth will die, 18 but I will confirm my covenant with you. You will enter the ark—you, your sons, your wife, and your sons' wives with you. 19 You must bring into the ark two of every kind of living creature from all flesh, male and female, to keep them alive with you. 20 Of the birds after their kinds, and of the cattle after their kinds, and of every creeping thing of the ground after its kind, two of every kind will come to you so you can keep them alive. 21 And you must take for yourself every kind of food that is eaten, and gather it together. It will be food for you and for them."

22 And Noah did all that God commanded him—he did indeed.

Hebrews 11:7

7 By faith Noah, when he was warned about things not yet seen, with reverent regard constructed an ark for the deliverance of his family. Through faith he condemned the world and became an heir of the righteousness that comes by faith.

SOAP / *Hebrews 11:7*
SCRIPTURE / *Write out the SOAP verses*

_____

_____

_____

_____

_____

_____

_____

_____

_____

_____

_____

_____

_____

_____

_____

_____

_____

OBSERVATION / *Write 3 - 4 observations*

_____

_____

_____

_____

_____

_____

APPLICATION / *Write down 1 - 2 applications*

_____
_____
_____
_____
_____
_____
_____
_____
_____
_____
_____

PRAYER / *Write out a prayer over what you learned*

_____
_____
_____
_____
_____
_____
_____
_____
_____
_____
_____
_____
_____
_____
_____
_____
_____

SOAP

Hebrews 11:7

By faith Noah, when he was warned about things not yet seen, with reverent regard constructed an ark for the deliverance of his family. Through faith he condemned the world and became an heir of the righteousness that comes by faith.

INTO THE TEXT

Noah found favor with God. While he is described as a godly man, blameless among his contemporaries, it was God alone who chose to show grace to Noah. Noah's faithfulness to God and willingness to follow God's commands stands in direct contrast to those around him. He lived in a wicked generation, yet he chose to walk with God. Enoch walked with God and was rewarded by being taken away; Noah followed Enoch's example and walked with God as well.

God commanded Noah to do something he had never seen. God warned Noah of what was to come, also something unheard of and unexpected. Though Noah may have had doubts, they are not recorded in Scripture. All we are told of is his faith.

Noah was willing to set aside what the world offered and follow God. He lived in righteousness and did all God commanded him. Noah is commended for his faith in Hebrews 11. Noah believed God existed and that God would reward him if he continued to walk with Him.

When we are faced with the unknown, do we turn to the security the world offers, or to God's commands? When we choose to step out in faith, we may not find worldly treasures or success, but we will find favor with God. Walking with God, honoring and following His commands, is how we exercise our faith and how we please Him.

PRAYER

Lord, I long to walk with You. Show me the areas in my life that do not honor You and bring You glory. Give me courage to cut these out of my life. Show me where my faith is lacking and increase my faith so I can continue to walk with You. Amen.

READ

Genesis 7:1-24

1 The LORD said to Noah, "Come into the ark, you and all your household, for I consider you godly among this generation. 2 You must take with you seven pairs of every kind of clean animal, the male and its mate, two of every kind of unclean animal, the male and its mate, 3 and also seven pairs of every kind of bird in the sky, male and female, to preserve their offspring on the face of the entire earth. 4 For in seven days I will cause it to rain on the earth for forty days and forty nights, and I will wipe from the face of the ground every living thing that I have made."

5 And Noah did all that the LORD commanded him.

6 Noah was 600 years old when the floodwaters engulfed the earth. 7 Noah entered the ark along with his sons, his wife, and his sons' wives because of the floodwaters. 8 Pairs of clean animals, of unclean animals, of birds, and of everything that creeps along the ground, 9 male and female, came into the ark to Noah, just as God had commanded him. 10 And after seven days the floodwaters engulfed the earth.

11 In the six hundredth year of Noah's life, in the second month, on the seventeenth day of the month—on that day all the fountains of the great deep burst open and the floodgates of the heavens were opened. 12 And the rain fell on the earth forty days and forty nights.

13 On that very day Noah entered the ark, accompanied by his sons Shem, Ham, and Japheth, along with his wife and his sons' three wives. 14 They entered, along with every living creature after its kind, every animal after its kind, every creeping thing that creeps on the earth after its kind, and every bird after its kind, everything with wings. 15 Pairs

Genesis 7:1-24 (continued)

of all creatures that have the breath of life came into the ark to Noah. 16 Those that entered were male and female, just as God commanded him. Then the LORD shut him in.

17 The flood engulfed the earth for forty days. As the waters increased, they lifted the ark and raised it above the earth. 18 The waters completely overwhelmed the earth, and the ark floated on the surface of the waters. 19 The waters completely inundated the earth so that even all the high mountains under the entire sky were covered. 20 The waters rose more than 20 feet above the mountains. 21 And all living things that moved on the earth died, including the birds, domestic animals, wild animals, all the creatures that swarm over the earth, and all humankind. 22 Everything on dry land that had the breath of life in its nostrils died. 23 So the LORD destroyed every living thing that was on the surface of the ground, including people, animals, creatures that creep along the ground, and birds of the sky. They were wiped off the earth. Only Noah and those who were with him in the ark survived. 24 The waters prevailed over the earth for 150 days.

Psalm 23
A psalm of David.

1 The LORD is my shepherd, I lack nothing. 2 He takes me to lush pastures, he leads me to refreshing water. 3 He restores my strength. He leads me down the right paths for the sake of his reputation. 4 Even when I must walk through the darkest valley, I fear no danger, for you are with me; your rod and your staff reassure me. 5 You prepare a feast before me in plain sight of my enemies. You refresh my head with oil; my cup is completely full. 6 Surely your goodness and faithfulness will pursue me all my days, and I will live in the LORD's house for the rest of my life.

"I said to the Lord, I'm going to hold steady on to you, and I know you will see me through"

Harriet Tubman

SOAP / *Psalm 23:4*
SCRIPTURE / *Write out the SOAP verses*

_____

_____

_____

_____

_____

_____

_____

_____

_____

_____

_____

_____

_____

_____

_____

_____

_____

_____

OBSERVATION / *Write 3 - 4 observations*

_____

_____

_____

_____

_____

_____

APPLICATION / *Write down 1 - 2 applications*

_____
_____
_____
_____
_____
_____
_____
_____
_____
_____

PRAYER / *Write out a prayer over what you learned*

_____
_____
_____
_____
_____
_____
_____
_____
_____
_____
_____
_____
_____
_____
_____

SOAP

Psalm 23:4

Even when I must walk through the darkest valley, I fear no danger, for you are with me; your rod and your staff reassure me.

INTO THE TEXT

Can you imagine what Noah may have felt when he and his family were in the middle of the flood? Noah had done everything God commanded him. He had been faithful to walk with God and he had been faithful in building the ark. God shut the door and the floods came. Noah and his family and the animals with them were all that survived. What a great sense of wonder and fear and confusion and anticipation they may have felt.

The same God who rescued Noah from a wicked generation, the same God who instructed Noah on exactly how to build the ark, the same God who shut the door, and the same God who protected Noah, his family, and the animals from the flood waters is still God today. He is with us in all our floods, all our valleys, all our fears.

Though God had destroyed all living creatures, He saved Noah and his family. God was with them, leading them even in the midst of darkness. We have all faced seasons of overwhelming fear. When we face valleys, whether from pain, loss, sin, fear, or oppression, our God is the same. He is the shepherd who cares for us. He is the One leading us to abundance, helping us when we are weak and tired, giving us strength and showing us the right path.

Noah had every reason to fear. He trusted God in the middle of his circumstances and walked with God day in and day out. May our lives be a reflection of Noah's, faithful to do all God has asked of us, faithful to cling to Him even in the darkest valley, and confident He is with us no matter what.

PRAYER

Father God, I know You are with me. You are my shepherd and I lack nothing in You. You are with me and I fear no danger. You assure me of who You are and what You can do. I trust You, Lord. Amen.

1. *Praise God for His character. Write Him a short hymn of praise, honoring Him for who He is and what He has done.*

....

....

....

2. *What does it mean to walk with God? How did Enoch walk with God? How can you walk with God in your daily life?*

....

....

....

3. *What does it mean to be justified by God's grace? Why is it just as important to remember that in Christ we are freely justified as it is to remember that all have sinned?*

....

....

....

4. *Why was Noah's faith so significant? Why is he commended in Hebrews 11 for his faith?*

....

....

....

5. *When has God been with you in the past in a season of darkness or difficulty? How does God's protection of Noah and his family give you comfort that God will protect you in future difficult seasons?*

....

....

....

And God said,
"This is the
guarantee of the
covenant I am
making with you
and every living
creature with you,
a covenant for
all subsequent
generations. I will
place my rainbow
in the clouds, and
it will become a
guarantee of the
covenant between
me and the earth.

Genesis 9:12–13

*Write down your prayer requests
and praises for this week.*

....

....

....

....

....

....

....

....

....

....

....

....

WEEKLY CHALLENGE

*God gave Noah a rainbow as a sign of His promise to never again destroy the whole
earth by a flood. Rainbows always follow a storm. What does this tell us about God's
care and provision for us in the midst of difficult times? How do you trust His
promises when you are in the middle of a storm?*

....

....

....

....

....

....

....

READ

Genesis 8:1-14

1 But God remembered Noah and all the wild animals and domestic animals that were with him in the ark. God caused a wind to blow over the earth and the waters receded. 2 The fountains of the deep and the floodgates of heaven were closed, and the rain stopped falling from the sky. 3 The waters kept receding steadily from the earth, so that they had gone down by the end of the 150 days. 4 On the seventeenth day of the seventh month, the ark came to rest on one of the mountains of Ararat. 5 The waters kept on receding until the tenth month. On the first day of the tenth month, the tops of the mountains became visible.

6 At the end of forty days, Noah opened the window he had made in the ark 7 and sent out a raven; it kept flying back and forth until the waters had dried up on the earth.

8 Then Noah sent out a dove to see if the waters had receded from the surface of the ground. 9 The dove could not find a resting place for its feet because water still covered the surface of the entire earth, and so it returned to Noah in the ark. He stretched out his hand, took the dove, and brought it back into the ark. 10 He waited seven more days and then sent out the dove again from the ark. 11 When the dove returned to him in the evening, there was a freshly plucked olive leaf in its beak! Noah knew that the waters had receded from the earth. 12 He waited another seven days and sent the dove out again, but it did not return to him this time.

13 In Noah's six hundred and first year, in the first day of the first month, the waters had dried up from the earth, and Noah removed the covering from the ark and saw that the surface of the ground was dry. 14 And by the twenty-seventh day of the second month the earth was dry.

Psalm 29:10-11

10 The LORD sits enthroned over the engulfing waters, the LORD sits enthroned as the eternal king. 11 The LORD gives his people strength; the LORD grants his people security.

SOAP / *Psalm 29:10-11*
SCRIPTURE / *Write out the SOAP verses*

_____

_____

_____

_____

_____

_____

_____

_____

_____

_____

_____

_____

_____

_____

_____

_____

_____

_____

OBSERVATION / *Write 3 - 4 observations*

_____

_____

_____

_____

_____

_____

APPLICATION / *Write down 1 - 2 applications*

_____

_____

_____

_____

_____

_____

_____

_____

_____

_____

PRAYER / *Write out a prayer over what you learned*

_____

_____

_____

_____

_____

_____

_____

_____

_____

_____

_____

_____

_____

_____

_____

SOAP

Psalm 29:10–11

The Lord sits enthroned over the engulfing waters, the Lord sits enthroned as the eternal king. The Lord gives his people strength; the Lord grants his people security.

INTO THE TEXT

God remembered Noah. God had certainly not forgotten Noah and his family while they were on the ark, so what does it mean that He remembered him? When God remembered Noah it meant His action changed. God had not forgotten him, but in His remembrance, He changed His action. When God remembered Noah He began to turn back the flood waters. The water began to recede and the earth started to dry up.

In the middle of a global flood, God remembered Noah. God caused the waters to recede so Noah and his family could again live on the earth. God was in control of that flood, and He is in control of the floods, either literal or metaphorical, that we face today.

The Hebrew word used for engulfing waters in Psalm 29 is the same word used in Genesis 8. If God was King of that flood, the one that destroyed all life on earth, then He is certainly King of your flood. He is enthroned over the engulfing waters of your emotions, your loneliness, your disaster, your fear, your needs, and your pain. When the floods come, we can remember His voice. No matter the strength or volume of the waters, God is King. He is enthroned over the waters. He is enthroned over all.

God remembers His people. He responds to them in their need. When we cry out to Him, He not only hears, He responds. He acts in accordance with His character. He is faithful, not only to hear and remember, but to respond. The God who remembered Noah remembers you and me. The God who commanded the waters to recede is working in your life today. He is the eternal King.

PRAYER

God, in Your great compassion, remember me. I need Your kindness and compassion to shower me today. I believe You are enthroned over all the floods I face. I believe You are faithful to hear my prayer and respond. Thank You for remembering me. Amen.

READ

Genesis 8:15-22

15 Then God spoke to Noah and said, 16 "Come out of the ark, you, your wife, your sons, and your sons' wives with you. 17 Bring out with you all the living creatures that are with you. Bring out every living thing, including the birds, animals, and every creeping thing that creeps on the earth. Let them increase and be fruitful and multiply on the earth!"

18 Noah went out along with his sons, his wife, and his sons' wives. 19 Every living creature, every creeping thing, every bird, and everything that moves on the earth went out of the ark in their groups.

20 Noah built an altar to the LORD. He then took some of every kind of clean animal and clean bird and offered burnt offerings on the altar. 21 And the LORD smelled the soothing aroma and said to himself, "I will never again curse the ground because of humankind, even though the inclination of their minds is evil from childhood on. I will never again destroy everything that lives, as I have just done.

22 "While the earth continues to exist, planting time and harvest, cold and heat, summer and winter, and day and night will not cease."

Psalm 115:16-18

16 The heavens belong to the LORD, but the earth he has given to mankind. 17 The dead do not praise the LORD, nor do any of those who descend into the silence of death. 18 But we will praise the LORD now and forevermore. Praise the LORD!

SOAP / *Psalm 115:16-18*
SCRIPTURE / *Write out the SOAP verses*

_____

_____

_____

_____

_____

_____

_____

_____

_____

_____

_____

_____

_____

_____

_____

_____

_____

_____

_____

OBSERVATION / *Write 3 - 4 observations*

_____

_____

_____

_____

_____

_____

_____

APPLICATION / *Write down 1 - 2 applications*

PRAYER / *Write out a prayer over what you learned*

SOAP

Psalm 115:16–18

The heavens belong to the Lord but the earth he has given to mankind. The dead do not praise the Lord, nor do any of those who descend into the silence of death. But we will praise the Lord now and forevermore. Praise the Lord!

INTO THE TEXT

After months of waiting, it was finally time for Noah and his family to leave the ark. As they left the ark God gave them the same command He gave Adam and Eve, to increase, to be fruitful, and to multiply on the earth.

The wickedness of humans had become so great, God needed to fully destroy the earth and begin again. Noah feared God, and Noah was the beginning of the new community God would establish, one that would worship Him. Noah's sacrifice to God pleased the Lord and He promised to never again destroy the whole earth, despite the sinfulness of humanity.

We were created to praise and honor God. We were designed to bring Him glory and make His name known. Instead, we have all turned to wickedness, desiring our own glory instead of God's. Yet, even in our rebellion, God saves us. He has showered us with mercy, not giving us what our sins deserve, and covered us with grace, giving us abundantly more than we could ever ask or think.

Unlike those who died in the flood, Noah could praise God. We have also been given the great privilege and pleasure of having access to God and the ability to praise Him. As Noah did, we can worship the Lord exactly where we are, no matter our circumstances. He alone is worthy of praise! Praise the Lord!

PRAYER

Lord, You are worthy of praise! I praise You for Your great mercy, for not treating me as my sins deserve, but allowing me to live and have a relationship with You. I am overwhelmed by Your grace that is beyond what I could image. Let my life be an outpouring of praise to You. Amen.

READ

Genesis 9:1-17

1 Then God blessed Noah and his sons and said to them, "Be fruitful and multiply and fill the earth. 2 Every living creature of the earth and every bird of the sky will be terrified of you. Everything that creeps on the ground and all the fish of the sea are under your authority. 3 You may eat any moving thing that lives. As I gave you the green plants, I now give you everything.

4 "But you must not eat meat with its life (that is, its blood) in it. 5 For your lifeblood I will surely exact punishment, from every living creature I will exact punishment. From each person I will exact punishment for the life of the individual since the man was his relative.

6 "Whoever sheds human blood, by other humans must his blood be shed; for in God's image God has made humankind.

7 "But as for you, be fruitful and multiply; increase abundantly on the earth and multiply on it."

8 God said to Noah and his sons, 9 "Look. I now confirm my covenant with you and your descendants after you 10 and with every living creature that is with you, including the birds, the domestic animals, and every living creature of the earth with you, all those that came out of the ark with you—every living creature of the earth. 11 I confirm my covenant with you: Never again will all living things be wiped out by the waters of a flood; never again will a flood destroy the earth."

12 And God said, "This is the guarantee of the covenant I am making with you and every living creature with you, a covenant for all subsequent generations: 13 I will place my rainbow in the clouds, and it will become a guarantee of the covenant between me and the earth. 14 Whenever I bring clouds over the earth and the rainbow appears in the clouds, 15 then I will remember my covenant with you and with all living creatures of all kinds. Never again will the waters become a flood and destroy all living things. 16 When the rainbow is in the clouds, I will notice it and remember the perpetual covenant between God and all living creatures of all kinds that are on the earth."

17 So God said to Noah, "This is the guarantee of the covenant that I am confirming between me and all living things that are on the earth."

2 Corinthians 1:20-22

20 For every one of God's promises are "Yes" in him; therefore also through him the "Amen" is spoken, to the glory we give to God. 21 But it is God who establishes us together with you in Christ and who anointed us, 22 who also sealed us and gave us the Spirit in our hearts as a down payment.

SOAP / *Genesis 9:12-13*
SCRIPTURE / *Write out the SOAP verses*

_____

_____

_____

_____

_____

_____

_____

_____

_____

_____

_____

_____

_____

_____

_____

_____

_____

_____

OBSERVATION / *Write 3 - 4 observations*

_____

_____

_____

_____

_____

_____

APPLICATION / *Write down 1 - 2 applications*

_____
_____
_____
_____
_____
_____
_____
_____
_____
_____

PRAYER / *Write out a prayer over what you learned*

_____
_____
_____
_____
_____
_____
_____
_____
_____
_____
_____
_____
_____
_____

SOAP

Genesis 9:12–13

And God said, "This is the guarantee of the covenant I am making with you and every living creature with you, a covenant for all subsequent generations: I will place my rainbow in the clouds, and it will become a guarantee of the covenant between me and the earth."

INTO THE TEXT

The covenant God made with Noah, the promise that God would never again kill all living things on earth by a flood, was the first recorded covenant God made with His people. This is an unconditional covenant. No matter the actions of humanity, God will never again destroy all life on the earth through a flood.

As a reminder of this covenant, God created the rainbow. He placed it in the clouds to remind Himself of His promise. The rainbow is not a reminder for God because He might forget. The same way God remembered Noah in the ark and changed His action, God sees His rainbow and is reminded of the everlasting covenant He made with humanity.

The rainbow is also a reminder to us. Rainbows only form when there is rain, and usually, after a rainstorm. Rainbows remind us that no matter how bad the storm, God keeps His promises. God will never again destroy the earth with a flood, and He will also keep all of His other promises to us.

The rainbow serves as a symbol of God's character. God is constant, never changing, and always faithful. He will never break His promises and He will always do what He says He will do. God's faithfulness in the past is a promise of His faithfulness in the future. His rainbow confirms that all His promises are yes in Christ.

PRAYER

Lord God, thank You for Your rainbow. Thank You for providing a reminder of Your character and Your promises to us every time it rains. Help me to be confident in all Your promises, even those I find hard to believe today. I trust Your character and Your promises. Amen.

READ

Genesis 9:18-29

18 The sons of Noah who came out of the ark were Shem, Ham, and Japheth. (Now Ham was the father of Canaan.) 19 These were the three sons of Noah, and from them the whole earth was populated.

20 Noah, a man of the soil, began to plant a vineyard. 21 When he drank some of the wine, he got drunk and uncovered himself inside his tent. 22 Ham, the father of Canaan, saw his father's nakedness and told his two brothers who were outside. 23 Shem and Japheth took the garment and placed it on their shoulders. Then they walked in backwards and covered up their father's nakedness. Their faces were turned the other way so they did not see their father's nakedness.

24 When Noah awoke from his drunken stupor he learned what his youngest son had done to him. 25 So he said, "Cursed be Canaan! The lowest of slaves he will be to his brothers."

26 He also said, "Worthy of praise is the Lord, the God of Shem! May Canaan be the slave of Shem! 27 May God enlarge Japheth's territory and numbers! May he live in the tents of Shem and may Canaan be the slave of Japheth!"

28 After the flood Noah lived 350 years. 29 The entire lifetime of Noah was 950 years, and then he died.

Exodus 13:3-5

3 Moses said to the people, "Remember this day on which you came out from Egypt, from the place where you were enslaved, for the Lord brought you out of there with a mighty hand—and no bread made with yeast may be eaten. 4 On this day, in the month of Abib, you are going out.

5 "When the Lord brings you to the land of the Canaanites, Hittites, Amorites, Hivites, and Jebusites, which he swore to your fathers to give you, a land flowing with milk and honey, then you will keep this ceremony in this month.

SOAP / *Genesis 9:26*
SCRIPTURE / *Write out the SOAP verses*

_____

_____

_____

_____

_____

_____

_____

_____

_____

_____

_____

_____

_____

_____

_____

_____

_____

_____

OBSERVATION / *Write 3 - 4 observations*

_____

_____

_____

_____

_____

_____

APPLICATION / *Write down 1 - 2 applications*

_____

_____

_____

_____

_____

_____

_____

_____

_____

_____

PRAYER / *Write out a prayer over what you learned*

_____

_____

_____

_____

_____

_____

_____

_____

_____

_____

_____

_____

_____

_____

SOAP

Genesis 9:26

He also said, "Worthy of praise is the Lord, the God of Shem! May Canaan be the slave of Shem!

INTO THE TEXT

Blessings and curses are a main theme in the book of Genesis. In Genesis chapter 9 Noah cursed his son Ham and blessed his sons Shem and Japheth. Ham's actions were improper and disrespectful while Shem and Japheth went out of their way to honor their father and protect his modesty.

In this moment God gave Noah insight into the future relations between his descendants. Moses, the largely undisputed author of Genesis, used this story to communicate the coming reputations and traits of the descendants of Noah's sons based on their actions. Shem was the ancestor to God's chosen people, the Israelites, while Ham's descendants became known as the Canaanites, whose land was handed over to the Israelites.

This story also offers us insight into how God wants those who follow Him to act. Shem and Japheth were blessed for honoring their father while Ham was cursed for his actions. God's people are to handle corruption according to His Word, not according to their own gains. The righteous conduct of Shem and Japheth was rewarded, not only in their lifetimes, but for their descendants as well.

Shem and Japheth's actions marked them as children of God. It was abundantly clear they had chosen to walk with God and honor His commands. Noah praised the Lord, calling Him "the God of Shem!" When we are in step with God's truth and walk daily in His commands, those around us will know who we serve. When we are in step with the Spirit we make God's name great.

PRAYER

Lord, You are God. I long for my life to be a testament to Your glory and goodness. Keep me from sin. Open my eyes to temptation and give me a way out. Allow me to live a life that honors You and glorifies Your name in all circumstances. You are worthy of praise, and I want to follow You and not the world. In Jesus' name, amen.

READ

Genesis 10:1-7

1 This is the account of Noah's sons: Shem, Ham, and Japheth. Sons were born to them after the flood.

2 The sons of Japheth were Gomer, Magog, Madai, Javan, Tubal, Meshech, and Tiras. 3 The sons of Gomer were Ashkenaz, Riphath, and Togarmah. 4 The sons of Javan were Elishah, Tarshish, the Kittim, and the Dodanim. 5 From these the coastlands of the nations were separated into their lands, every one according to its language, according to their families, by their nations.

6 The sons of Ham were Cush, Mizraim, Put, and Canaan. 7 The sons of Cush were Seba, Havilah, Sabtah, Raamah, and Sabteca. The sons of Raamah were Sheba and Dedan.

Acts 17:26

26 From one man he made every nation of the human race to inhabit the entire earth, determining their set times and the fixed limits of the places where they would live,

SOAP / *Acts 17:26*
SCRIPTURE / *Write out the SOAP verses*

OBSERVATION / *Write 3 - 4 observations*

APPLICATION / *Write down 1 - 2 applications*

PRAYER / *Write out a prayer over what you learned*

SOAP

Acts 17:26

From one man he made every nation of the human race to inhabit the entire earth, determining their set times and the fixed limits of the places where they would live.

INTO THE TEXT

When Paul visited Athens, he was greatly disturbed by the number of idols he saw there. He even saw an altar "to an unknown god." Paul stood up in front of the people and began to explain to them who this unknown god was, how it was in fact, the God of creation, the Lord of heaven and earth. Paul explained how this God had created the earth in its entirety, including all of the human race. God had specifically chosen for each person the time and place where they should live in order that they would search for and find God.

When we read genealogies in Scripture it is easy to become distracted or indifferent to the information they contain. However, when we look closely, we gain a much clearer picture of the purpose and intent of God in creating humans. God had an incredible plan when He created the earth; everything was made for a specific purpose, with specific intention to bring glory to God. Humanity is no different. God has a specific plan for each person, family, community, and nation. He knows all and He specifically places them in both the times and places where they are to live.

What an awesome God! That He not only knows us intimately, but that even before we were born, He chose when and where we would live. These people mentioned in Genesis became families, clans, and nations that greatly impacted the world with culture, industry, and art, both for good and for evil. While many choose to turn from Him, God is still in control and sovereign over each member of the human race. He desires that none should perish, but that all would come to Him. No matter when or where we live, God has a plan and a purpose for our lives and for His glory.

PRAYER

Father God, You have created me with a specific plan and purpose for making Your name known. Show me how I can glorify and honor You today. Help me be a light to those around me that I may point them to Your Son, Jesus Christ. Amen.

1. *How does Psalm 29:10-11 remind us of God's sovereignty?*

....

....

....

2. *Why is it important for us to praise God? Does God need our praise? Why does God ask us to praise Him?*

....

....

....

3. *How does the rainbow remind us of God's faithfulness? What other signs of His faithfulness has God given you?*

....

....

....

4. *How has God fulfilled His promises in your life? What themes or promises keep coming up in your walk of faith that remind you of God's faithfulness?*

....

....

....

5. *How does Acts 17:26 give you comfort? If God knew when and where you would live, how can you rest no matter what lays before you today?*

....

....

....

Your (eyes) saw me when I was inside the womb. All the days ordained for me were recorded in your scroll before one of them came into existence.

Psalm 139:16

*Write down your prayer requests
and praises for this week.*

....

....

....

....

....

....

....

....

....

....

....

....

WEEKLY CHALLENGE

*Read Psalm 139 this week. Meditate and reflect on God's full knowledge of you. He
knows you inside and out and still loves you. Spend time this week reflecting on this
truth. Ask Him to show you His peace as you rest in the truth that He knows you
fully and completely and loves you perfectly!*

....

....

....

....

....

....

WEEK 6
Monday

READ

Genesis 10:8-20

8 Cush was the father of Nimrod; he began to be a valiant warrior on the earth. 9 He was a mighty hunter before the LORD. (That is why it is said, "Like Nimrod, a mighty hunter before the LORD.") 10 The primary regions of his kingdom were Babel, Erech, Akkad, and Calneh in the land of Shinar. 11 From that land he went to Assyria, where he built Nineveh, Rehoboth Ir, Calah, 12 and Resen, which is between Nineveh and the great city Calah.

13 Mizraim was the father of the Ludites, Anamites, Lehabites, Naphtuhites, 14 Pathrusites, Casluhites (from whom the Philistines came), and Caphtorites.

15 Canaan was the father of Sidon his firstborn, Heth, 16 the Jebusites, Amorites, Girgashites, 17 Hivites, Arkites, Sinites, 18 Arvadites, Zemarites, and Hamathites. Eventually the families of the Canaanites were scattered 19 and the borders of Canaan extended from Sidon all the way to Gerar as far as Gaza, and all the way to Sodom, Gomorrah, Admah, and Zeboyim, as far as Lasha. 20 These are the sons of Ham, according to their families, according to their languages, by their lands, and by their nations.

Jonah 3

1 The LORD's message came to Jonah a second time, 2 "Go immediately to Nineveh, that large city, and proclaim to it the message that I tell you." 3 So Jonah went immediately to Nineveh, in keeping with the LORD's message. Now Nineveh was an enormous city—it required three days to walk through it! 4 Jonah began to enter the city by going one day's walk, announcing, "At the end of forty days, Nineveh will be overthrown!"

5 The people of Nineveh believed in God, and they declared a fast and put on sackcloth, from the greatest to the least of them. 6 When the news reached the king of Nineveh, he got up from his throne, took off his royal robe, put on sackcloth, and sat on ashes. 7 He issued a proclamation and said, "In Nineveh, by the decree of the king and his nobles: No human or animal, cattle or sheep, is to taste anything; they must not eat and they must not drink water. 8 Every person and animal must put on sackcloth and must cry earnestly to God, and everyone must turn from their evil way of living and from the violence that they do. 9 Who knows? Perhaps God might be willing to change his mind and relent and turn from his fierce anger so that we might not die." 10 When God saw their actions—that they turned from their evil way of living.—God relented concerning the judgment he had threatened them with and did not destroy them.

SOAP / *Jonah 3:10*
SCRIPTURE / *Write out the SOAP verses*

_____

_____

_____

_____

_____

_____

_____

_____

_____

_____

_____

_____

_____

_____

_____

_____

_____

OBSERVATION / *Write 3 - 4 observations*

_____

_____

_____

_____

_____

_____

APPLICATION / *Write down 1 - 2 applications*

PRAYER / *Write out a prayer over what you learned*

SOAP

Jonah 3:10

When God saw their actions—that they turned from their evil way of living—God relented concerning the judgment he had threatened them with and did not destroy them.

INTO THE TEXT

As Noah's family repopulated the earth, some people followed God while some turned from Him. Nimrod was a mighty hunter who ruled a large kingdom. He built the city of Nineveh, a city in the Assyrian Empire that was known for violence and wickedness. The prophet Jonah traveled to Nineveh, preaching God's message. Jonah was reluctant to go to Nineveh and tell the people to repent, not because he was afraid for his life, but because he feared God's compassion. Jonah hated the Ninevites and wanted God to completely and utterly destroy them, not show them compassion.

The people of Nineveh turned (though only for a time) from their wickedness. God relented from His planned destruction and did not bring judgment on the city. His compassion astounded the people of Nineveh, but Jonah was not surprised. Jonah wanted to see his enemy destroyed and he was (at least initially) upset by God's compassion.

Years later, the city of Nineveh had turned back to their wicked ways. The prophet Nahum spoke of God's promised destruction on the city of Nineveh for their blatant rebellion against God and their wickedness toward God's people. God destroyed the city of Nineveh and the rest of the Assyrians with it.

The legacy of the city of Nineveh reminds us of the vastness of God's character. He is in control and His actions may be beyond our understanding. Whether He chooses to show grace to the wicked or to enact vengeance, His character remains the same. His goodness and holiness are displayed through His work whether we believe it fits our own interests or not. But we can trust Him. He created the earth, He chose and selected each person and the time and place for them to live. He has a plan and purpose, and we can trust His character.

PRAYER

Lord God, help me trust Your character. I believe You are good, not only to me, but to all You have made. I know I can trust Your actions even if I do not understand them. Help me believe You are always working for Your glory and my good, and help me to rest in Your matchless kindness, compassion, and love. Amen.

READ

Genesis 10:21-32

21 And sons were also born to Shem (the older brother of Japheth), the father of all the sons of Eber.

22 The sons of Shem were Elam, Asshur, Arphaxad, Lud, and Aram. 23 The sons of Aram were Uz, Hul, Gether, and Mash. 24 Arphaxad was the father of Shelah, and Shelah was the father of Eber. 25 Two sons were born to Eber: One was named Peleg because in his days the earth was divided, and his brother's name was Joktan. 26 Joktan was the father of Almodad, Sheleph, Hazarmaveth, Jerah, 27 Hadoram, Uzal, Diklah, 28 Obal, Abimael, Sheba, 29 Ophir, Havilah, and Jobab. All these were sons of Joktan. 30 Their dwelling place was from Mesha all the way to Sephar in the eastern hills. 31 These are the sons of Shem according to their families, according to their languages, by their lands, and according to their nations.

32 These are the families of the sons of Noah, according to their genealogies, by their nations, and from these the nations spread over the earth after the flood.

Proverbs 19:23

23 Fearing the LORD leads to life, and one who does so will live satisfied; he will not be afflicted by calamity.

SOAP / *Proverbs 19:23*
SCRIPTURE / *Write out the SOAP verses*

_____

_____

_____

_____

_____

_____

_____

_____

_____

_____

_____

_____

_____

_____

_____

_____

_____

_____

_____

OBSERVATION / *Write 3 - 4 observations*

_____

_____

_____

_____

_____

_____

_____

APPLICATION / *Write down 1 - 2 applications*

_____
_____
_____
_____
_____
_____
_____
_____
_____
_____

PRAYER / *Write out a prayer over what you learned*

_____
_____
_____
_____
_____
_____
_____
_____
_____
_____
_____
_____
_____
_____
_____
_____

SOAP

Proverbs 19:23

Fearing the Lord leads to life, and one who does so will live satisfied; he will not be afflicted by calamity.

INTO THE TEXT

One of the main themes of Genesis is the importance of fearing the Lord. When people feared God, they were given blessings and life. When they turned from and rebelled against God, they faced judgment or destruction. The author of Genesis made this clear in the account of Enoch, showing how his faithfulness to God kept him from even dying a physical death. Those who feared and followed God, like Abel, Noah, and Shem, were blessed while those who rebelled against God, like Cain and Ham, were cursed and received judgment.

The notion of fearing God means more than reverence or awe. It does indeed mean we are to *fear* Him. For people like Noah, fearing the Lord meant literally fearing Him. Noah had seen what God was capable of and what He could do to those who turned from Him. Noah feared God. Noah also had a relationship with God.

When we fear God we do indeed fear His wrath on our sin. But the fear of God also leads to an understanding of His character. God showers His people (and even His enemies, like Nineveh) with compassion and love. He longs to have a relationship with us. Our relationship with Him leads us to know His love, which drives out fear (1 Jn 4:18).

The fear of the Lord leads to life, and a satisfied life. Fearing God does not mean life will be full of material blessings, perfect days, and healthy bodies. Fearing God means we are satisfied in Him and Him alone in whatever circumstance we find ourselves. Fearing God leads to knowing Him. When we know and understand His love, we are blessed by His presence.

PRAYER

Lord, I do fear You. As Your child, I want to follow You, not only because I understand the greatness of Your wrath, but because I have come to know the great love You lavish on me. You are full of compassion and mercy. Help me be fully satisfied in You. Amen.

READ

Genesis 11:1-9

11 The whole earth had a common language and a common vocabulary. 2 When the people moved eastward, they found a plain in Shinar and settled there. 3 Then they said to one another, "Come, let's make bricks and bake them thoroughly." (They had brick instead of stone and tar instead of mortar.) 4 Then they said, "Come, let's build ourselves a city and a tower with its top in the heavens so that we may make a name for ourselves. Otherwise we will be scattered across the face of the entire earth."

5 But the LORD came down to see the city and the tower that the people had started building. 6 And the LORD said, "If as one people all sharing a common language they have begun to do this, then nothing they plan to do will be beyond them. 7 Come, let's go down and confuse their language so they won't be able to understand each other."

8 So the LORD scattered them from there across the face of the entire earth, and they stopped building the city. 9 That is why its name was called Babel—because there the LORD confused the language of the entire world, and from there the LORD scattered them across the face of the entire earth.

Isaiah 55:8-9

8 "Indeed, my plans are not like your plans, and my deeds are not like your deeds," says the LORD, 9 "for just as the sky is higher than the earth, so my deeds are superior to your deeds and my plans superior to your plans.

SOAP / *Isaiah 55:8-9*
SCRIPTURE / *Write out the SOAP verses*

_____

_____

_____

_____

_____

_____

_____

_____

_____

_____

_____

_____

_____

_____

_____

_____

_____

_____

_____

_____

OBSERVATION / *Write 3 - 4 observations*

_____

_____

_____

_____

_____

_____

_____

APPLICATION / *Write down 1 - 2 applications*

PRAYER / *Write out a prayer over what you learned*

SOAP

Isaiah 55:8–9

"Indeed, my plans are not like your plans, and my deeds are not like your deeds," says the Lord, "for just as the sky is higher than the earth, so my deeds are superior to your deeds and my plans superior to your plans."

INTO THE TEXT

When the people in the earth settled in Shinar they set out to build a tower and a city for their own fame. Their desire was to remain together in one place where they would gain fame and be known throughout the world. They intended to remain exactly where they had settled, directly rebelling against God's command to fill the entire earth.

God stopped the people in their tracks, confusing their language, forcing them to scatter from one another. They were forced to spread out, living in new places because they could not understand one another. This allowed God to fulfill His purpose for humanity, to fill the whole earth. Their pride led them to disobedience against God as they sought to make themselves known above God.

God's actions in this story can sound harsh, scattering families and communities, divided by language. But God had a grand plan and purpose for humanity, one that humans directly disobeyed. God's command for them was to scatter and fill the earth, to make His name and power known. Instead of focusing on God's glory, they sought their own.

While God's actions may not always make sense to us, we can rest assured that He is still in control. His plans and actions may shock us, like acquitting a wicked city or scattering people across the earth. They are not our plans. But when God's actions don't make sense to us, we can find peace and assurance in His character. He is good, holy, powerful, compassionate, merciful, gracious, and full of love. Regardless of His actions, we can be confident that His character never changes.

PRAYER

Lord God, I trust Your plans. Help me trust You when I do not understand Your actions. Your ways are higher than mine. When I am confused by Your actions, show me more of Your character. Help me trust You even when I don't understand what You are doing. Amen.

READ

Genesis 11:10-26

10 This is the account of Shem.

Shem was 100 years old when he became the father of Arphaxad, two years after the flood. 11 And after becoming the father of Arphaxad, Shem lived 500 years and had other sons and daughters.

12 When Arphaxad had lived 35 years, he became the father of Shelah. 13 And after he became the father of Shelah, Arphaxad lived 403 years and had other sons and daughters.

14 When Shelah had lived 30 years, he became the father of Eber. 15 And after he became the father of Eber, Shelah lived 403 years and had other sons and daughters.

16 When Eber had lived 34 years, he became the father of Peleg. 17 And after he became the father of Peleg, Eber lived 430 years and had other sons and daughters.

18 When Peleg had lived 30 years, he became the father of Reu. 19 And after he became the father of Reu, Peleg lived 209 years and had other sons and daughters.

20 When Reu had lived 32 years, he became the father of Serug. 21 And after he became the father of Serug, Reu lived 207 years and had other sons and daughters.

22 When Serug had lived 30 years, he became the father of Nahor. 23 And after he became the father of Nahor, Serug lived 200 years and had other sons and daughters.

24 When Nahor had lived 29 years, he became the father of Terah. 25 And after he became the father of Terah, Nahor lived 119 years and had other sons and daughters.

26 When Terah had lived 70 years, he became the father of Abram, Nahor, and Haran.

Matthew 1:1-17

1 This is the record of the genealogy of Jesus Christ, the son of David, the son of Abraham.

2 Abraham was the father of Isaac, Isaac the father of Jacob, Jacob the father of Judah and his brothers, 3 Judah the father of Perez and Zerah (by Tamar), Perez the father of Hezron, Hezron the father of Ram, 4 Ram the father of Amminadab, Amminadab the father of Nahshon, Nahshon the father of Salmon, 5 Salmon the father of Boaz (by Rahab), Boaz the father of Obed (by Ruth), Obed the father of Jesse, 6 and Jesse the father of David the king.

David was the father of Solomon (by the wife of Uriah), 7 Solomon the father of Rehoboam, Rehoboam the father of Abijah, Abijah the father of Asa, 8 Asa the father of Jehoshaphat, Jehoshaphat the father of Joram, Joram the father of Uzziah, 9 Uzziah the father of Jotham, Jotham the father of Ahaz, Ahaz the father of Hezekiah, 10 Hezekiah the father of Manasseh, Manasseh the father of Amon, Amon the father of Josiah, 11 and Josiah the father of Jeconiah and his brothers, at the time of the deportation to Babylon.

12 After the deportation to Babylon, Jeconiah became the father of Shealtiel, Shealtiel the father of Zerubbabel, 13 Zerubbabel the father of Abiud, Abiud the father of Eliakim, Eliakim the father of Azor, 14 Azor the father of Zadok, Zadok the father of Achim, Achim the father of Eliud, 15 Eliud the father of Eleazar, Eleazar the father of Matthan, Matthan the father of Jacob, 16 and Jacob the father of Joseph, the husband of Mary, by whom Jesus was born, who is called Christ.

17 So all the generations from Abraham to David are fourteen generations, and from David to the deportation to Babylon, fourteen generations, and from the deportation to Babylon to Christ, fourteen generations.

"Wanted: More Praise I cannot help believing that the world will be a better and a happier place when people are praised more and blamed less..."

Frances Willard

SOAP / *Matthew 1:16*
SCRIPTURE / *Write out the SOAP verses*

_____

_____

_____

_____

_____

_____

_____

_____

_____

_____

_____

_____

_____

_____

_____

_____

_____

_____

OBSERVATION / *Write 3 - 4 observations*

_____

_____

_____

_____

_____

_____

_____

APPLICATION / *Write down 1 - 2 applications*

_____

_____

_____

_____

_____

_____

_____

_____

_____

_____

PRAYER / *Write out a prayer over what you learned*

_____

_____

_____

_____

_____

_____

_____

_____

_____

_____

_____

_____

_____

_____

_____

SOAP

Matthew 1:16

and Jacob the father of Joseph, the husband of Mary, by whom Jesus was born, who is called Christ.

INTO THE TEXT

The Book of Genesis was written by Moses during the forty years the Israelites wandered in the desert. The book was written to a generation of Israelites who were about to enter the Promised Land of Canaan. Many of these Israelites had been born into slavery in Egypt, but many of them were also born during the wilderness wanderings. Those who knew of Egypt had been young when they left, spending most of their lives waiting for God to fulfill His promise and bring them into the land.

These first chapters of Genesis describe the way the earth was created and the first people who inhabited it. An Israelite reading the genealogy in Genesis 11 would have recognized the names of those mentioned from the stories they had been told. God had given a promise to Abram, and these Israelites knew they were the fruit of that promise.

When we read the genealogy in the book of Matthew today, we have a similar perspective as the Israelites did when Moses wrote Genesis. The Israelites knew who Abram was, what he would do, and who his children would become. When we read the genealogy of Jesus, we know who He is, what He did, and what would become of His followers.

The Israelites read Genesis 11 knowing God had already fulfilled part of His promise. He had made Abram a great nation, but part of the promise was still to come: the inheritance of the land. When we see the life of Jesus we know God has already fulfilled part of His promise: He sent Jesus, the Messiah, who took away the sins of the world. Today, we wait for God to fulfill the rest of His promise: Christ's return and reign. Our God is the same God. He is the Promise Maker and the Promise Keeper. He kept His promise to Abram and He will indeed keep His promise to us.

PRAYER

Lord God, You are the Promise Keeper. You promised to send Your Son as the Messiah, to save us from sin. You have done it. I believe in Your promise, that Jesus will come again to judge and rule. Thank You for showing me Your promise keeping character over and over again in Your Word. Amen.

READ

Genesis 11:27-32

27 This is the account of Terah.

Terah became the father of Abram, Nahor, and Haran. And Haran became the father of Lot. 28 Haran died in the land of his birth, in Ur of the Chaldeans, while his father Terah was still alive. 29 And Abram and Nahor took wives for themselves. The name of Abram's wife was Sarai. And the name of Nahor's wife was Milcah; she was the daughter of Haran, who was the father of both Milcah and Iscah. 30 But Sarai was barren; she had no children.

31 Terah took his son Abram, his grandson Lot (the son of Haran), and his daughter-in-law Sarai, his son Abram's wife, and with them he set out from Ur of the Chaldeans to go to Canaan. When they came to Haran, they settled there. 32 The lifetime of Terah was 205 years, and he died in Haran.

Psalm 139:13-16

13 Certainly you made my mind and heart; you wove me together in my mother's womb. 14 I will give you thanks because your deeds are awesome and amazing. You knew me thoroughly; 15 my bones were not hidden from you, when I was made in secret and sewed together in the depths of the earth. 16 Your eyes saw me when I was inside the womb. All the days ordained for me were recorded in your scroll before one of them came into existence.

SOAP / *Psalm 139:16*
SCRIPTURE / *Write out the SOAP verses*

_____

_____

_____

_____

_____

_____

_____

_____

_____

_____

_____

_____

_____

_____

_____

_____

_____

_____

OBSERVATION / *Write 3 - 4 observations*

_____

_____

_____

_____

_____

_____

_____

APPLICATION / *Write down 1 - 2 applications*

_____

_____

_____

_____

_____

_____

_____

_____

_____

_____

PRAYER / *Write out a prayer over what you learned*

_____

_____

_____

_____

_____

_____

_____

_____

_____

_____

_____

_____

_____

_____

SOAP

Psalm 139:16

Your eyes saw me when I was inside the womb. All the days ordained for me were recorded in your scroll before one of them came into existence.

INTO THE TEXT

The Book of Genesis describes the origins of God's people. Chapters 1–11 describe the way God created the heavens and the earth and everything in them. They display the power of God in creation, the wrath of God against sin, and the compassion of God for His people. They also show God's incredible, intricate, detailed plan for humanity.

God planned to bring humanity into the world, knowing they would rebel against Him. Even from the beginning, God planned and orchestrated our redemption. He established a family and then a nation who would be His representatives in the world. Genesis 1–11 introduces this family, the family of Abram, and foreshadows God's redemptive plan.

The themes in Genesis 1–11 allow us to wrestle with the character of God. Sometimes, God did things we didn't understand. Sometimes, God did exactly what we hoped He would do. Sometimes, God went above and beyond to shower His people with grace and mercy. God works the same way in our lives today. We are able to come to Him with our questions, ask Him for forgiveness, seek His compassion, and rest in His love.

God saw the earth before it was formed. God saw the family of Abram, the ancestor of the Messiah, before He had created a single human. God sees us in our lives today. He knows the intimate details of who we are and what we need. He has ordained all of our days, the places and times where we live, and what we would think and do before one of them came to be. We can trust a God like that. We can rest in His character and His promises even when we are overwhelmed with questions. He is gracious and compassionate, slow to anger and rich in faithful love.

PRAYER

Lord God, I am amazed at Your works. I am amazed at Your power, Your compassion, Your love, and Your justice. Help me trust You when I do not understand Your actions. Help me believe You when my world seems to fall apart. Help me rest in Your presence. You have ordained all my days. I love You, Lord. In Jesus' name, amen.

1. *How is God's compassion displayed in Jonah 3? Why would God offer grace to those who rejected Him and tormented His people?*

....

....

....

2. *What does it mean to fear the Lord? How does this bring us life rather than destruction?*

....

....

....

3. *Does Isaiah 55:8-9 give you comfort or fear? Why do you think it causes this reaction in you? Why is it important to surrender our lives and plans to God?*

....

....

....

4. *What can we learn by studying the genealogies in the Bible? Why do you think God wanted us to know the history and family lines of His people?*

....

....

....

5. *Does Psalm 139 bring you comfort or anxiety? Are you glad God knows all of your actions and days, or do you wish He didn't know everything about you? Why?*

....

....

....

bridge

SOAP it up between studies
2 week reading plan

Have you developed a consistent, daily Bible study habit
and don't want to break it before our next study begins?
In the following pages, you can continue your quiet
time with our suggested reading and SOAP passages.

WEEK 1

○ *Monday*
Read: Psalm 61–62
SOAP: Psalm 61:1–2

○ *Tuesday*
Read: Psalm 63–64
SOAP: Psalm 63:3–5

○ *Wednesday*
Read: Psalm 65–66
SOAP: Psalm 66:19–20

○ *Thursday*
Read: Psalm 67–68
SOAP: Psalm 68:5–6

○ *Friday*
Read: Psalm 69–70
SOAP: Psalm 69:13–14

WEEK 2

○ *Monday*
Read: Psalm 71–72
SOAP: Psalm 71:20–21

○ *Tuesday*
Read: Psalm 73–74
SOAP: Psalm 73:26

○ *Wednesday*
Read: Psalm 75–76
SOAP: Psalm 76:11–12

○ *Thursday*
Read: Psalm 77–78
SOAP: Psalm 77:11–12

○ *Friday*
Read: Psalm 79–80
SOAP: Psalm 79:8

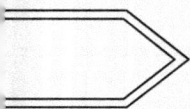

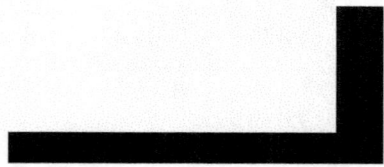

God deserves praise, for he did not reject my prayer or abandon his love for me.

Psalm 66:20

PRAY

*Write down your prayer requests
and praises for this week.*

....
....
....
....
....
....
....
....
....
....
....
....
....
....
....
....
....
....
....
....
....
....
....
....
....
....
....

Psalm 61

*For the music director, to be played on a
stringed instrument; written by David.*

1 O God, hear my cry for help.
Pay attention to my prayer.
2 From the remotest place on earth
I call out to you in my despair.
Lead me up to a rocky summit where I can be safe.
3 Indeed, you are my shelter,
a strong tower that protects me from the enemy.
4 I will be a permanent guest in your home;
I will find shelter in the protection
of your wings. (Selah)
5 For you, O God, hear my vows;
you grant me the reward that belongs
to your loyal followers.
6 Give the king long life.
Make his lifetime span several generations.
7 May he reign forever before God.
Decree that your loyal love and
faithfulness should protect him.
8 Then I will sing praises to
your name continually,
as I fulfill my vows day after day.

Psalm 62

For the music director, Jeduthun; a psalm of David.

1 For God alone I patiently wait;
he is the one who delivers me.
2 He alone is my protector and deliverer.
He is my refuge; I will not be upended.
3 How long will you threaten a man like me?
All of you are murderers,
as dangerous as a leaning wall or an unstable fence.
4 They spend all their time planning
how to bring their victim down.
They love to use deceit;
they pronounce blessings with their mouths,
but inwardly they utter curses. (Selah)
5 Patiently wait for God alone, my soul!
For he is the one who gives me hope.
6 He alone is my protector and deliverer.
He is my refuge; I will not be shaken.
7 God delivers me and exalts me;
God is my strong protector and my shelter.
8 Trust in him at all times, you people!
Pour out your hearts before him.
God is our shelter. (Selah)
9 Men are nothing but a mere breath;
human beings are unreliable.
When they are weighed in the scales,
all of them together are lighter than air.
10 Do not trust in what you can gain by oppression.
Do not put false confidence in what
you can gain by robbery.
If wealth increases, do not become attached to it.
11 God has declared one principle;
two principles I have heard:
God is strong,
12 and you, O LORD, demonstrate loyal love.
For you repay men for what they do.

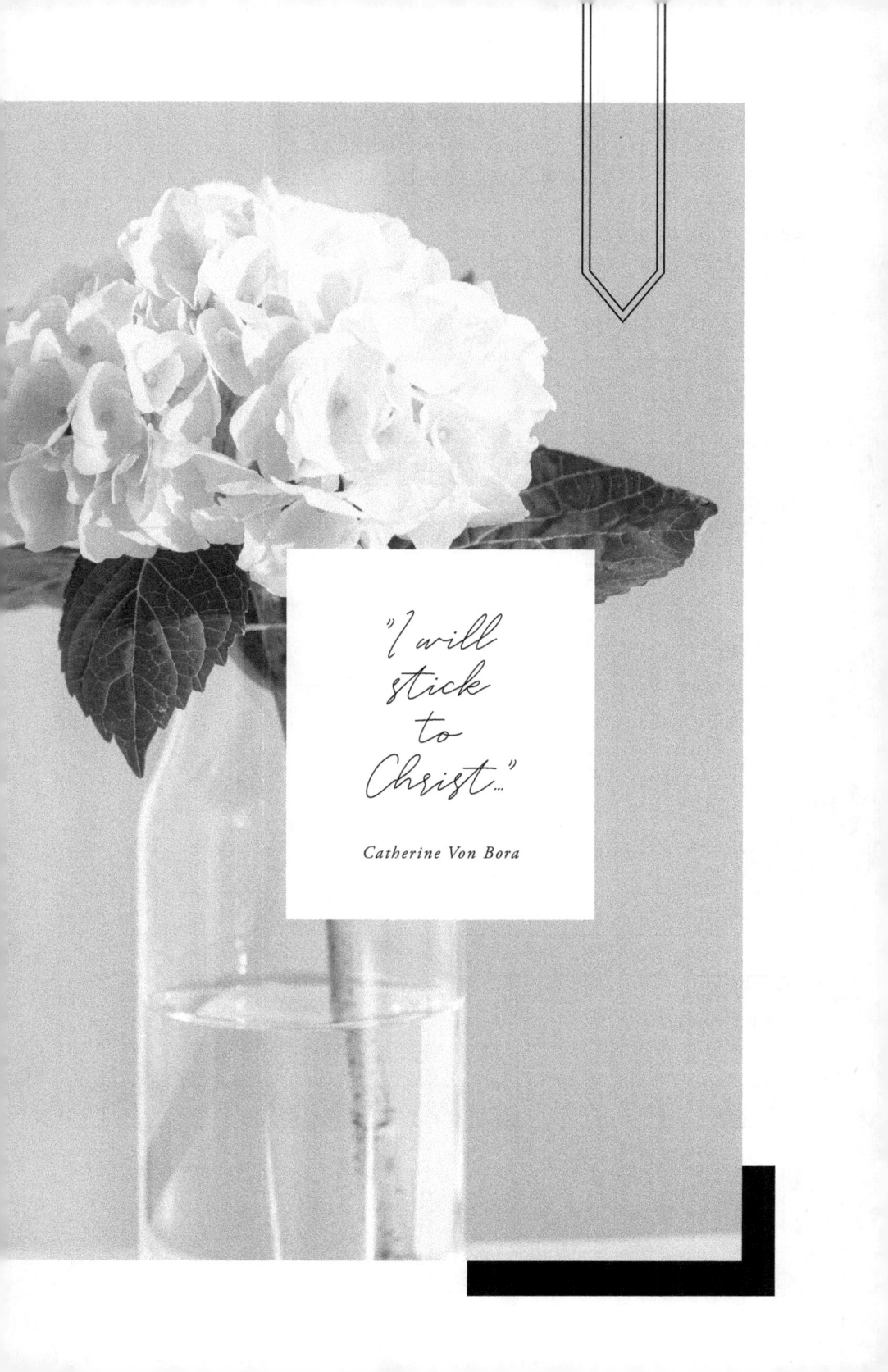

"I will stick to Christ..."

Catherine Von Bora

SOAP / *Psalm 61:1–2*
SCRIPTURE / *Write out the SOAP verses*

_____
_____
_____
_____
_____
_____
_____
_____
_____
_____
_____
_____
_____
_____
_____
_____
_____
_____
_____

OBSERVATION / *Write 3 - 4 observations*

_____
_____
_____
_____
_____
_____
_____

APPLICATION / *Write down 1 - 2 applications*

_____

_____

_____

_____

_____

_____

_____

_____

_____

_____

PRAYER / *Write out a prayer over what you learned*

_____

_____

_____

_____

_____

_____

_____

_____

_____

_____

_____

_____

_____

_____

_____

THANKFUL

*Write three things you are thankful for
today and why each one brings you joy.*

ONE

....

....

....

....

....

....

....

TWO

....

....

....

....

....

....

....

THREE

....

....

....

....

....

....

....

Psalm 63

*A psalm of David, written when he
was in the Judean wilderness.*

1 O God, you are my God. I long for you.
My soul thirsts for you,
my flesh yearns for you,
in a dry and parched land where there is no water.
2 Yes, in the sanctuary I have seen you,
and witnessed your power and splendor.
3 Because experiencing your loyal
love is better than life itself,
my lips will praise you.
4 For this reason I will praise you while I live;
in your name I will lift up my hands.
5 As with choice meat you satisfy my soul.
My mouth joyfully praises you,
6 whenever I remember you on my bed,
and think about you during the nighttime hours.
7 For you are my deliverer;
under your wings I rejoice.
8 My soul pursues you;
your right hand upholds me.
9 Enemies seek to destroy my life,
but they will descend into the depths of the earth.
10 Each one will be handed over to the sword;
their corpses will be eaten by jackals.
11 But the king will rejoice in God;
everyone who takes oaths in his name will boast,
for the mouths of those who speak lies will be shut up.

Psalm 64

For the music director, a psalm of David.

1 Listen to me, O God, as I offer my lament!
Protect my life from the enemy's
terrifying attacks.
2 Hide me from the plots of evil men,
from the crowd of evildoers.
3 They sharpen their tongues like swords;
they aim their arrows, a slanderous charge,
4 in order to shoot down the
innocent in secluded places.
They shoot at him suddenly and
are unafraid of retaliation.
5 They encourage one another to
carry out their evil deed.
They plan how to hide snares,
and boast, "Who will see them?"
6 They devise unjust schemes;
they disguise a well-conceived plot.
Man's inner thoughts cannot be discovered.
7 But God will shoot at them;
suddenly they will be wounded by an arrow.
8 Their slander will bring about their demise.
All who see them will shudder,
9 and all people will fear.
They will proclaim what God has done,
and reflect on his deeds.
10 The godly will rejoice in the LORD
and take shelter in him.
All the morally upright will boast.

"I began to discover a beauty in the way of salvation by Christ. He appeared to be just such a Saviour as I needed."

Ann Haseltine Judson

SOAP / *Psalm 63:3–5*
SCRIPTURE / *Write out the SOAP verses*

_____

_____

_____

_____

_____

_____

_____

_____

_____

_____

_____

_____

_____

_____

_____

_____

_____

_____

_____

OBSERVATION / *Write 3 - 4 observations*

_____

_____

_____

_____

_____

_____

_____

APPLICATION / *Write down 1 - 2 applications*

_____
_____
_____
_____
_____
_____
_____
_____
_____
_____
_____

PRAYER / *Write out a prayer over what you learned*

_____
_____
_____
_____
_____
_____
_____
_____
_____
_____
_____
_____
_____
_____
_____
_____

THANKFUL

*Write three things you are thankful for
today and why each one brings you joy.*

ONE

....
....
....
....
....
....
....

TWO

....
....
....
....
....
....
....

THREE

....
....
....
....
....
....
....

Psalm 65

For the music director, a psalm of David, a song.

1 Praise awaits you, O God, in Zion.
Vows made to you are fulfilled.
2 You hear prayers;
all people approach you.
3 Our record of sins overwhelms me,
but you forgive our acts of rebellion.
4 How blessed is the one whom you choose,
and allow to live in your palace courts.
May we be satisfied with the good things of your house—
your holy palace.
5 You answer our prayers by performing
awesome acts of deliverance,
O God, our savior.
All the ends of the earth trust in you,
as well as those living across the wide seas.
6 You created the mountains by your power,
and demonstrated your strength.
7 You calmed the raging seas
and their roaring waves,
as well as the commotion made by the nations.
8 Even those living in the remotest
areas are awestruck by your acts;
you cause those living in the east and west to praise you.
9 You visit the earth and give it rain;
you make it rich and fertile.
God's streams are full of water;
you provide grain for the people of the earth,
for you have prepared the earth in this way.
10 You saturate its furrows,
and soak its plowed ground.
With rain showers you soften its soil,
and make its crops grow.
11 You crown the year with your good blessings,
and you leave abundance in your wake.
12 The pastures in the wilderness glisten with moisture,
and the hills are clothed with joy.
13 The meadows are clothed with sheep,
and the valleys are covered with grain.
They shout joyfully, yes, they sing.

Psalm 66

For the music director, a song, a psalm.

1 Shout out praise to God, all the earth!
2 Sing praises about the
majesty of his reputation.
Give him the honor he deserves!
3 Say to God:
"How awesome are your deeds!
Because of your great power your
enemies cower in fear before you.
4 All the earth worships you
and sings praises to you.
They sing praises to your name." (Selah)
5 Come and witness God's exploits!
His acts on behalf of
people are awesome.
6 He turned the sea into dry land;
they passed through the river on foot.
Let us rejoice in him there.
7 He rules by his power forever;
he watches the nations.
Stubborn rebels should not
exalt themselves. (Selah)
8 Praise our God, you nations.
Loudly proclaim his praise.
9 He preserves our lives
and does not allow our feet to slip.
10 For you, O God, tested us;
you purified us like refined silver.

Psalm 66 (continued)

11 You led us into a trap;
you caused us to suffer.
12 You allowed men to
ride over our heads;
we passed through fire and water,
but you brought us out into
a wide open place.
13 I will enter your temple
with burnt sacrifices;
I will fulfill the vows I made to you,
14 which my lips uttered
and my mouth spoke when
I was in trouble.
15 I will offer up to you fattened
animals as burnt sacrifices,
along with the smell of sacrificial rams.
I will offer cattle and goats. (Selah)
16 Come! Listen, all you
who are loyal to God.
I will declare what he has done for me.
17 I cried out to him for help
and praised him with my tongue.
18 If I had harbored sin in my heart,
the LORD would not have listened.
19 However, God heard;
he listened to my prayer.
20 God deserves praise,
for he did not reject my prayer
or abandon his love for me.

SOAP / *Psalm 66:19–20*
SCRIPTURE / *Write out the SOAP verses*

_____

_____

_____

_____

_____

_____

_____

_____

_____

_____

_____

_____

_____

_____

_____

_____

_____

_____

OBSERVATION / *Write 3 - 4 observations*

_____

_____

_____

_____

_____

_____

APPLICATION / *Write down 1 - 2 applications*

_____

_____

_____

_____

_____

_____

_____

_____

_____

_____

PRAYER / *Write out a prayer over what you learned*

_____

_____

_____

_____

_____

_____

_____

_____

_____

_____

_____

_____

_____

_____

_____

THANKFUL

*Write three things you are thankful for
today and why each one brings you joy.*

ONE

....
....
....
....
....
....
....

TWO

....
....
....
....
....
....
....

THREE

....
....
....
....
....
....
....

Psalm 67

For the music director, to be accompanied
by stringed instruments; a psalm, a song.

1 May God show us his favor and bless us.
May he smile on us. (Selah)
2 Then those living on earth will
know what you are like;
all nations will know how you deliver your people.
3 Let the nations thank you, O God.
Let all the nations thank you.
4 Let foreigners rejoice and celebrate.
For you execute justice among the nations,
and govern the people living on earth. (Selah)
5 Let the nations thank you, O God.
Let all the nations thank you.
6 The earth yields its crops.
May God, our God, bless us.
7 May God bless us.
Then all the ends of the earth will
give him the honor he deserves.

Psalm 68

For the music director, by David, a psalm, a song.

1 God springs into action.
His enemies scatter;
his adversaries run from him.
2 As smoke is driven away by the
wind, so you drive them away.
As wax melts before fire,
so the wicked are destroyed before God.
3 But the godly are happy;
they rejoice before God
and are overcome with joy.
4 Sing to God! Sing praises to his name.
Exalt the one who rides on the clouds.
For the LORD is his name.
Rejoice before him.
5 He is a father to the fatherless
and an advocate for widows.

Psalm 68 (continued)

God rules from his holy dwelling place.
6 God settles in their own homes those who have been deserted;
he frees prisoners and grants them prosperity.
But sinful rebels live in the desert.
7 O God, when you lead your people into battle,
when you march through the wastelands, (Selah)
8 the earth shakes.
Yes, the heavens pour down rain
before God, the God of Sinai,
before God, the God of Israel.
9 O God, you cause abundant showers to fall on your chosen people.
When they are tired, you sustain them,
10 for you live among them.
You sustain the oppressed with your good blessings, O God.
11 The LORD speaks;
many, many women spread the good news.
12 Kings leading armies run away—they run away!
The lovely lady of the house divides up the loot.
13 When you lie down among the sheepfolds,
the wings of the dove are covered with silver
and with glittering gold.
14 When the Sovereign One scatters kings,
let it snow on Zalmon.
15 The mountain of Bashan is a towering mountain;
the mountain of Bashan is a mountain with many peaks.
16 Why do you look with envy, O mountains with many peaks,
at the mountain where God has decided to live?
Indeed the LORD will live there permanently.
17 God has countless chariots;
they number in the thousands.
The LORD comes from Sinai in holy splendor.
18 You ascend on high;
you have taken many captives.
You receive tribute from men,
including even sinful rebels.
Indeed, the LORD God lives there.
19 The LORD deserves praise.
Day after day he carries our burden,
the God who delivers us. (Selah)
20 Our God is a God who delivers;
the LORD, the Sovereign LORD, can rescue from death.

Psalm 68 (continued)

21 Indeed, God strikes the heads of his enemies,
the hairy foreheads of those who persist in rebellion.
22 The LORD says,
"I will retrieve them from Bashan.
I will bring them back from the depths of the sea,
23 so that your feet may stomp in their blood,
and your dogs may eat their portion of the enemies' corpses."
24 They see your processions, O God—
the processions of my God, my king, who
marches along in holy splendor.
25 Singers walk in front;
musicians follow playing their stringed instruments,
in the midst of young women playing tambourines.
26 In your large assemblies praise God,
the LORD, in the assemblies of Israel.
27 There is little Benjamin, their ruler,
and the princes of Judah in their robes,
along with the princes of Zebulun and the princes of Naphtali.
28 God has decreed that you will be powerful.
O God, you who have acted on our
behalf, demonstrate your power.
29 Because of your temple in Jerusalem,
kings bring tribute to you.
30 Sound your battle cry against the wild beast of the reeds,
and the nations that assemble like a herd of calves led by bulls.
They humble themselves and offer gold and silver as tribute.
God scatters the nations that like to do battle.
31 They come with red cloth from Egypt.
Ethiopia voluntarily offers tribute to God.
32 O kingdoms of the earth, sing to God.
Sing praises to the LORD, (Selah)
33 to the one who rides through the sky from ancient times.
Look! He thunders loudly.
34 Acknowledge God's power,
his sovereignty over Israel,
and the power he reveals in the skies.
35 You are awe-inspiring, O God, as you
emerge from your holy temple.
It is the God of Israel who gives the
people power and strength.
God deserves praise!

SOAP / *Psalm 68:5–6*
SCRIPTURE / *Write out the SOAP verses*

_____

_____

_____

_____

_____

_____

_____

_____

_____

_____

_____

_____

_____

_____

_____

_____

_____

_____

OBSERVATION / *Write 3 - 4 observations*

_____

_____

_____

_____

_____

_____

_____

APPLICATION / *Write down 1 - 2 applications*

PRAYER / *Write out a prayer over what you learned*

THANKFUL

WEEK 1 • THURSDAY

*Write three things you are thankful for
today and why each one brings you joy.*

ONE

....

....

....

....

....

....

....

TWO

....

....

....

....

....

....

....

THREE

....

....

....

....

....

....

....

Psalm 69

*For the music director, according to
the tune of "Lilies"; by David.*

1 Deliver me, O God,
for the water has reached my neck.
2 I sink into the deep mire
where there is no solid ground;
I am in deep water,
and the current overpowers me.
3 I am exhausted from shouting for help.
My throat is sore;
my eyes grow tired from looking for my God.
4 Those who hate me without cause
are more numerous than the hairs of my head.
Those who want to destroy me,
my enemies for no reason,
outnumber me.
They make me repay what I did not steal.
5 O God, you are aware of my foolish sins;
my guilt is not hidden from you.
6 Let none who rely on you be disgraced because of me,
O Sovereign Lord of Heaven's Armies.
Let none who seek you be ashamed because of me,
O God of Israel.
7 For I suffer humiliation for your sake
and am thoroughly disgraced.
8 My own brothers treat me like a stranger;
they act as if I were a foreigner.
9 Certainly zeal for your house consumes me;
I endure the insults of those who insult you.
10 I weep and refrain from eating food,
which causes others to insult me.
11 I wear sackcloth
and they ridicule me.
12 Those who sit at the city gate gossip about me;
drunkards mock me in their songs.
13 O Lord, may you hear my prayer
and be favorably disposed to me.

Psalm 69 (continued)

O God, because of your great loyal love,
answer me with your faithful deliverance.
14 Rescue me from the mud. Don't let me sink.
Deliver me from those who hate me,
from the deep water.
15 Don't let the current overpower me.
Don't let the deep swallow me up.
Don't let the Pit devour me.
16 Answer me, O Lord, for your loyal love is good.
Because of your great compassion, turn toward me.
17 Do not ignore your servant,
for I am in trouble. Answer me right away.
18 Come near me and redeem me.
Because of my enemies, rescue me.
19 You know how I am insulted,
humiliated, and disgraced;
you can see all my enemies.
20 Their insults are painful and make me lose heart;
I look for sympathy, but receive none,
for comforters, but find none.
21 They put bitter poison into my food,
and to quench my thirst they give me vinegar to drink.
22 May their dining table become a trap before them.
May it be a snare for that group of friends.
23 May their eyes be blinded.
Make them shake violently.
24 Pour out your judgment on them.
May your raging anger overtake them.
25 May their camp become desolate,
their tents uninhabited.
26 For they harass the one whom you discipline;
they spread the news about the suffering
of those whom you punish.
27 Hold them accountable for all their sins.
Do not vindicate them.
28 May their names be deleted from
the scroll of the living.
Do not let their names be listed with the godly.
29 I am oppressed and suffering.
O God, deliver and protect me.

Psalm 69 (continued)

30 I will sing praises to God's name.
I will magnify him as I give him thanks.
31 That will please the LORD more than an ox or a bull
with horns and hooves.
32 The oppressed look on—let them rejoice.
You who seek God, may you be encouraged.
33 For the LORD listens to the needy;
he does not despise his captive people.
34 Let the heavens and the earth praise him,
along with the seas and everything that swims in them.
35 For God will deliver Zion
and rebuild the cities of Judah,
and his people will again live in
them and possess Zion.
36 The descendants of his servants will inherit it,
and those who are loyal to him will live in it.

Psalm 70

For the music director, by David;
written to get God's attention.

1 O God, please be willing to rescue me.
O LORD, hurry and help me.
2 May those who are trying to take my life
be embarrassed and ashamed.
May those who want to harm me
be turned back and ashamed.
3 May those who say, "Aha! Aha!"
be driven back and disgraced.
4 May all those who seek you be
happy and rejoice in you.
May those who love to experience your
deliverance say continually,
"May God be praised!"
5 I am oppressed and needy.
O God, hurry to me.
You are my helper and my deliverer.
O LORD, do not delay.

SOAP / *Psalm 69:13–14*
SCRIPTURE / *Write out the SOAP verses*

_____

_____

_____

_____

_____

_____

_____

_____

_____

_____

_____

_____

_____

_____

_____

_____

_____

_____

OBSERVATION / *Write 3 - 4 observations*

_____

_____

_____

_____

_____

_____

APPLICATION / *Write down 1 - 2 applications*

PRAYER / *Write out a prayer over what you learned*

*Write three things you are thankful for
today and why each one brings you joy.*

ONE

....
....
....
....
....
....
....

TWO

....
....
....
....
....
....
....

THREE

....
....
....
....
....
....
....

REFLECT

Record an application you learned from your SOAP study this week and how you will practically implement it in your life.

....
....
....
....
....
....
....
....
....
....
....
....
....
....
....
....
....
....
....
....
....
....
....
....
....
....

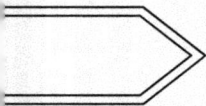

My flesh and my heart may grow weak, but God always protects my heart and gives me stability.

Psalm 73:26

Write down your prayer requests and praises for this week.

....

....

....

....

....

....

....

....

....

....

....

....

....

....

....

....

....

....

....

....

....

....

....

....

....

Psalm 71

1 In you, O Lord, I have taken shelter.
Never let me be humiliated.
2 Vindicate me by rescuing me.
Listen to me. Deliver me.
3 Be my protector and refuge,
a stronghold where I can be safe.
For you are my high ridge and my stronghold.
4 My God, rescue me from the power of the wicked,
from the hand of the cruel oppressor.
5 For you are my hope;
O Sovereign Lord, I have trusted
in you since I was young.
6 I have leaned on you since birth;
you pulled me from my mother's womb.
I praise you continually.
7 Many are appalled when they see me,
but you are my secure shelter.
8 I praise you constantly
and speak of your splendor all day long.
9 Do not reject me in my old age.
When my strength fails, do not abandon me.
10 For my enemies talk about me;
those waiting for a chance to kill me plot my demise.
11 They say, "God has abandoned him.
Run and seize him, for there is no
one who will rescue him."
12 O God, do not remain far away from me.
My God, hurry and help me.
13 May my accusers be humiliated and defeated.
May those who want to harm me be
covered with scorn and disgrace.
14 As for me, I will wait continually,
and will continue to praise you.
15 I will tell about your justice,
and all day long proclaim your salvation,
though I cannot fathom its full extent.
16 I will come and tell about the mighty
acts of the Sovereign Lord.
I will proclaim your justice—yours alone.
17 O God, you have taught me since I was young,
and I am still declaring your amazing deeds.

Psalm 71 (continued)

18 Even when I am old and gray,
O God, do not abandon me,
until I tell the next generation about your strength,
and those coming after me about your power.
19 Your justice, O God, extends to the skies above;
you have done great things.
O God, who can compare to you?
20 Though you have allowed me to
experience much trouble and distress,
revive me once again.
Bring me up once again from the depths of the earth.
21 Raise me to a position of great honor.
Turn and comfort me.
22 I will express my thanks to you
with a stringed instrument,
praising your faithfulness, O my God.
I will sing praises to you accompanied by a harp,
O Holy One of Israel.
23 My lips will shout for joy. Yes, I will sing your praises.
I will praise you when you rescue me.
24 All day long my tongue will also tell about your justice,
for those who want to harm me will
be embarrassed and ashamed.

Psalm 72

For Solomon.

1 O God, grant the king the ability to make just decisions.
Grant the king's son the ability to make fair decisions.
2 Then he will judge your people fairly,
and your oppressed ones equitably.
3 The mountains will bring news of peace to the people,
and the hills will announce justice.
4 He will defend the oppressed among the people;
he will deliver the children of the poor
and crush the oppressor.
5 People will fear you as long as the sun
and moon remain in the sky,
for generation after generation.

Psalm 72 (Continued)

6 He will descend like rain on the mown grass,
like showers that drench the earth.
7 During his days the godly will flourish;
peace will prevail as long as the moon remains in the sky.
8 May he rule from sea to sea,
and from the Euphrates River to the ends of the earth.
9 Before him the coastlands will bow down,
and his enemies will lick the dust.
10 The kings of Tarshish and the
coastlands will offer gifts;
the kings of Sheba and Seba will bring tribute.
11 All kings will bow down to him;
all nations will serve him.
12 For he will rescue the needy
when they cry out for help,
and the oppressed who have no defender.
13 He will take pity on the poor and needy;
the lives of the needy he will save.
14 From harm and violence he will defend them;
he will value their lives.
15 May he live! May they offer him gold from Sheba.
May they continually pray for him.
May they pronounce blessings on him all day long.
16 May there be an abundance of grain in the earth;
on the tops of the mountains may it sway.
May its fruit trees flourish like the forests of Lebanon.
May its crops be as abundant as the grass of the earth.
17 May his fame endure.
May his dynasty last as long as the
sun remains in the sky.
May they use his name when they
formulate their blessings.
May all nations consider him to be favored by God.
18 The LORD God, the God of Israel, deserves praise.
He alone accomplishes amazing things.
19 His glorious name deserves praise forevermore.
May his majestic splendor fill the whole earth.
We agree! We agree!
20 This collection of the prayers of
David son of Jesse ends here.

SOAP / *Psalm 71:20–21*
SCRIPTURE / *Write out the SOAP verses*

_____

_____

_____

_____

_____

_____

_____

_____

_____

_____

_____

_____

_____

_____

_____

_____

_____

OBSERVATION / *Write 3 - 4 observations*

_____

_____

_____

_____

_____

_____

APPLICATION / *Write down 1 - 2 applications*

_____

_____

_____

_____

_____

_____

_____

_____

_____

_____

PRAYER / *Write out a prayer over what you learned*

_____

_____

_____

_____

_____

_____

_____

_____

_____

_____

_____

_____

_____

THANKFUL

WEEK 2 · MONDAY

*Write three things you are thankful for
today and why each one brings you joy.*

ONE

....
....
....
....
....
....
....

TWO

....
....
....
....
....
....
....

THREE

....
....
....
....
....
....
....

Psalm 73

A psalm by Asaph.

1 Certainly God is good to Israel,
and to those whose motives are pure.
2 But as for me, my feet almost slipped;
my feet almost slid out from under me.
3 For I envied those who are proud,
as I observed the prosperity of the wicked.
4 For they suffer no pain;
their bodies are strong and well fed.
5 They are immune to the trouble common to men;
they do not suffer as other men do.
6 Arrogance is their necklace,
and violence covers them like clothing.
7 Their prosperity causes them to do wrong;
their thoughts are sinful.
8 They mock and say evil things;
they proudly threaten violence.
9 They speak as if they rule in heaven,
and lay claim to the earth.
10 Therefore they have more than enough food to eat,
and even suck up the water of the sea.
11 They say, "How does God know what we do?
Is the Most High aware of what goes on?"
12 Take a good look. This is what the wicked are like,
those who always have it so easy and get richer and richer.
13 I concluded, "Surely in vain I
have kept my motives pure
and maintained a pure lifestyle.
14 I suffer all day long,
and am punished every morning."
15 If I had publicized these thoughts,
I would have betrayed your people.
16 When I tried to make sense of this,
it was troubling to me.
17 Then I entered the precincts of God's temple,
and understood the destiny of the wicked.
18 Surely you put them in slippery places;
you bring them down to ruin.
19 How desolate they become in a mere moment.
Terrifying judgments make their demise complete.

Psalm 73 (continued)

20 They are like a dream after one wakes up.
O Lord, when you awake you will despise them.
21 Yes, my spirit was bitter,
and my insides felt sharp pain.
22 I was ignorant and lacked insight;
I was as senseless as an animal before you.
23 But I am continually with you;
you hold my right hand.
24 You guide me by your wise advice,
and then you will lead me to a position of honor.
25 Whom do I have in heaven but you?
On earth there is no one I desire but you.
26 My flesh and my heart may grow weak,
but God always protects my heart and gives me stability.
27 Yes, look! Those far from you die;
you destroy everyone who is unfaithful to you.
28 But as for me, God's presence is all I need.
I have made the Sovereign Lord my shelter,
as I declare all the things you have done.

Psalm 74

A well-written song by Asaph.

1 Why, O God, have you permanently rejected us?
Why does your anger burn against
the sheep of your pasture?
2 Remember your people whom you
acquired in ancient times,
whom you rescued so they could be your very own nation,
as well as Mount Zion, where you dwell.
3 Hurry to the permanent ruins,
and to all the damage the enemy has done to the temple.
4 Your enemies roar in the middle of your sanctuary;
they set up their battle flags.
5 They invade like lumberjacks
swinging their axes in a thick forest.
6 And now they are tearing down all its engravings
with axes and crowbars.
7 They set your sanctuary on fire;

Psalm 74 (continued)

they desecrate your dwelling place
by knocking it to the ground.
8 They say to themselves,
"We will oppress all of them."
They burn down all the places in the
land where people worship God.
9 We do not see any signs of God's presence;
there are no longer any prophets,
and we have no one to tell us how long this will last.
10 How long, O God, will the adversary hurl insults?
Will the enemy blaspheme your name forever?
11 Why do you remain inactive?
Intervene and destroy him.
12 But God has been my king from ancient times,
performing acts of deliverance on the earth.
13 You destroyed the sea by your strength;
you shattered the heads of the
sea monster in the water.
14 You crushed the heads of Leviathan;
you fed him to the people who live along the coast.
15 You broke open the spring and the stream;
you dried up perpetually flowing rivers.
16 You established the cycle of day and night;
you put the moon and sun in place.
17 You set up all the boundaries of the earth;
you created the cycle of summer and winter.
18 Remember how the enemy hurls insults, O Lord,
and how a foolish nation blasphemes your name.
19 Do not hand the life of your
dove over to a wild animal.
Do not continue to disregard the
lives of your oppressed people.
20 Remember your covenant promises,
for the dark regions of the earth are full
of places where violence rules.
21 Do not let the afflicted be turned back in shame.
Let the oppressed and poor praise your name.
22 Rise up, O God. Defend your honor.
Remember how fools insult you all day long.
23 Do not disregard what your enemies say,
or the unceasing shouts of those who defy you.

SOAP / *Psalm 73:26*
SCRIPTURE / *Write out the SOAP verses*

_____

_____

_____

_____

_____

_____

_____

_____

_____

_____

_____

_____

_____

_____

_____

_____

_____

_____

OBSERVATION / *Write 3 - 4 observations*

_____

_____

_____

_____

_____

_____

APPLICATION / *Write down 1 - 2 applications*

_____
_____
_____
_____
_____
_____
_____
_____
_____
_____

PRAYER / *Write out a prayer over what you learned*

_____
_____
_____
_____
_____
_____
_____
_____
_____
_____
_____
_____
_____
_____
_____

THANKFUL

Write three things you are thankful for today and why each one brings you joy.

ONE

....

....

....

....

....

....

....

TWO

....

....

....

....

....

....

....

THREE

....

....

....

....

....

....

....

Psalm 75

*For the music director, according to the
al-tashcheth style; a psalm of Asaph, a song.*

1 We give thanks to you, O God. We give thanks.
You reveal your presence;
people tell about your amazing deeds.
2 God says,
"At the appointed times,
I judge fairly.
3 When the earth and all its inhabitants dissolve in fear,
I make its pillars secure." (Selah)
4 I say to the proud, "Do not be proud,"
and to the wicked, "Do not be so confident of victory.
5 Do not be so certain you have won.
Do not speak with your head held so high.
6 For victory does not come from the east or west,
or from the wilderness.
7 For God is the judge.
He brings one down and exalts another.
8 For the LORD holds in his hand a cup
full of foaming wine mixed with spices,
and pours it out.
Surely all the wicked of the earth
will slurp it up and drink it to its very last drop."
9 As for me, I will continually tell what you have done;
I will sing praises to the God of Jacob.
10 God says,
"I will bring down all the power of the wicked;
the godly will be victorious."

Psalm 76

*For the music director, to be accompanied by
stringed instruments; a psalm of Asaph, a song.*

1 God has revealed himself in Judah;
in Israel his reputation is great.
2 He lives in Salem;
he dwells in Zion.
3 There he shattered the arrows,
the shield, the sword, and the rest of
the weapons of war. (Selah)
4 You shine brightly and reveal your majesty,
as you descend from the hills where you killed your prey.
5 The bravehearted were plundered;
they "fell asleep."
All the warriors were helpless.
6 At the sound of your battle cry, O God of Jacob,
both rider and horse "fell asleep."
7 You are awesome! Yes, you!
Who can withstand your intense anger?
8 From heaven you announced what
their punishment would be.
The earth was afraid and silent
9 when God arose to execute judgment,
and to deliver all the oppressed of the earth. (Selah)
10 Certainly your angry judgment
upon men will bring you praise;
you reveal your anger in full measure.
11 Make vows to the LORD your God and repay them.
Let all those who surround him bring
tribute to the awesome one.
12 He humbles princes;
the kings of the earth regard him as awesome.

"Here was I worrying about my journey, while God was helping me all the way."

Gladys Aylward

SOAP / *Psalm 76:11–12*
SCRIPTURE / *Write out the SOAP verses*

_____

_____

_____

_____

_____

_____

_____

_____

_____

_____

_____

_____

_____

_____

_____

_____

_____

OBSERVATION / *Write 3 - 4 observations*

_____

_____

_____

_____

_____

APPLICATION / *Write down 1 - 2 applications*

PRAYER / *Write out a prayer over what you learned*

THANKFUL

*Write three things you are thankful for
today and why each one brings you joy.*

ONE

....
....
....
....
....
....
....

TWO

....
....
....
....
....
....
....

THREE

....
....
....
....
....
....
....

Psalm 77

For the music director, Jeduthun; a psalm of Asaph.

1 I will cry out to God and call for help.
I will cry out to God and he will pay attention to me.
2 In my time of trouble I sought the LORD.
I kept my hand raised in prayer throughout the night.
I refused to be comforted.
3 I said, "I will remember God while I groan;
I will think about him while my
strength leaves me." (Selah)
4 You held my eyelids open;
I was troubled and could not speak.
5 I thought about the days of old,
about ancient times.
6 I said, "During the night I will
remember the song I once sang;
I will think very carefully."
I tried to make sense of what was happening.
7 I asked, "Will the LORD reject me forever?
Will he never again show me his favor?
8 Has his loyal love disappeared forever?
Has his promise failed forever?
9 Has God forgotten to be merciful?
Has his anger stifled his compassion?" (Selah)
10 Then I said, "I am sickened by the thought
that the Most High might become inactive.
11 I will remember the works of the LORD.
Yes, I will remember the amazing things you did long ago.
12 I will think about all you have done;
I will reflect upon your deeds."
13 O God, your deeds are extraordinary.
What god can compare to our great God?
14 You are the God who does amazing things;
you have revealed your strength among the nations.
15 You delivered your people by your strength—
the children of Jacob and Joseph. (Selah)
16 The waters saw you, O God,
the waters saw you and trembled.
Yes, the depths of the sea shook with fear.
17 The clouds poured down rain;
the skies thundered.

Psalm 77 (continued)

Yes, your arrows flashed about.
18 Your thunderous voice was heard in the wind;
the lightning bolts lit up the world.
The earth trembled and shook.
19 You walked through the sea;
you passed through the surging waters,
but left no footprints.
20 You led your people like a flock of sheep,
by the hand of Moses and Aaron.

Psalm 78

A well-written song by Asaph.

1 Pay attention, my people, to my instruction.
Listen to the words I speak.
2 I will sing a song that imparts wisdom;
I will make insightful observations about the past.
3 What we have heard and learned—
that which our ancestors have told us—
4 we will not hide from their descendants.
We will tell the next generation
about the LORD's praiseworthy acts,
about his strength and the amazing things he has done.
5 He established a rule in Jacob;
he set up a law in Israel.
He commanded our ancestors
to make his deeds known to their descendants,
6 so that the next generation, children yet to be born,
might know about them.
They will grow up and tell their descendants about them.
7 Then they will place their confidence in God.
They will not forget the works of God,
and they will obey his commands.
8 Then they will not be like their ancestors,
who were a stubborn and rebellious generation,
a generation that was not committed
and faithful to God.
9 The Ephraimites were armed with bows,
but they retreated in the day of battle.

Psalm 78 (continued)

10 They did not keep their covenant with God,
and they refused to obey his law.
11 They forgot what he had done,
the amazing things he had shown them.
12 He did amazing things in the sight of their ancestors,
in the land of Egypt, in the region of Zoan.
13 He divided the sea and led them across it;
he made the water stand in a heap.
14 He led them with a cloud by day,
and with the light of a fire all night long.
15 He broke open rocks in the wilderness,
and gave them enough water to fill the depths of the sea.
16 He caused streams to flow from the rock,
and made the water flow like rivers.
17 Yet they continued to sin against him,
and rebelled against the Most High in the desert.
18 They willfully challenged God
by asking for food to satisfy their appetite.
19 They insulted God, saying,
"Is God really able to give us food in the wilderness?
20 Yes, he struck a rock and water flowed out;
streams gushed forth.
But can he also give us food?
Will he provide meat for his people?"
21 When the LORD heard this, he was furious.
A fire broke out against Jacob,
and his anger flared up against Israel,
22 because they did not have faith in God,
and did not trust his ability to deliver them.
23 He gave a command to the clouds above,
and opened the doors in the sky.
24 He rained down manna for them to eat;
he gave them the grain of heaven.
25 Man ate the food of the mighty ones.
He sent them more than enough to eat.
26 He brought the east wind through the sky,
and by his strength led forth the south wind.
27 He rained down meat on them like dust,
birds as numerous as the sand on the seashores.

Psalm 78 (continued)

28 He caused them to fall right in
the middle of their camp,
all around their homes.
29 They ate until they were beyond full;
he gave them what they desired.
30 They were not yet filled up;
their food was still in their mouths,
31 when the anger of God flared up against them.
He killed some of the strongest of them;
he brought the young men of Israel to their knees.
32 Despite all this, they continued to sin,
and did not trust him to do amazing things.
33 So he caused them to die unsatisfied
and filled with terror.
34 When he struck them down, they sought his favor;
they turned back and longed for God.
35 They remembered that God was their protector,
and that God Most High was their deliverer.
36 But they deceived him with their words,
and lied to him.
37 They were not really committed to him,
and they were unfaithful to his covenant.
38 Yet he is compassionate.
He forgives sin and does not destroy.
He often holds back his anger,
and does not stir up his fury.
39 He remembered that they were made of flesh,
and were like a wind that blows past and does not return.
40 How often they rebelled against him in the wilderness,
and insulted him in the wastelands.
41 They again challenged God,
and offended the Holy One of Israel.
42 They did not remember what he had done,
how he delivered them from the enemy,
43 when he performed his awesome deeds in Egypt,
and his acts of judgment in the region of Zoan.
44 He turned their rivers into blood,
and they could not drink from their streams.

Psalm 78 (continued)

45 He sent swarms of biting insects against them,
as well as frogs that overran their land.
46 He gave their crops to the grasshopper,
the fruit of their labor to the locust.
47 He destroyed their vines with hail,
and their sycamore-fig trees with driving rain.
48 He rained hail down on their cattle,
and hurled lightning bolts down on their livestock.
49 His raging anger lashed out against them.
He sent fury, rage, and trouble
as messengers who bring disaster.
50 He sent his anger in full force.
He did not spare them from death;
he handed their lives over to destruction.
51 He struck down all the firstborn in Egypt,
the firstfruits of their reproductive
power in the tents of Ham.
52 Yet he brought out his people like sheep;
he led them through the wilderness like a flock.
53 He guided them safely along, and they were not afraid;
but the sea covered their enemies.
54 He brought them to the border of his holy land,
to this mountainous land that his right hand acquired.
55 He drove the nations out from before them;
he assigned them their tribal allotments
and allowed the tribes of Israel to settle down.
56 Yet they challenged and defied God Most High,
and did not obey his commands.
57 They were unfaithful and acted as
treacherously as their ancestors;
they were as unreliable as a malfunctioning bow.
58 They made him angry with their pagan shrines,
and made him jealous with their idols.
59 God heard and was angry;
he completely rejected Israel.
60 He abandoned the sanctuary at Shiloh,
the tent where he lived among men.

Psalm 78 (continued)

61 He allowed the symbol of his
strong presence to be captured;
he gave the symbol of his splendor
into the hand of the enemy.
62 He delivered his people over to the sword,
and was angry with his chosen nation.
63 Fire consumed their young men,
and their virgins remained unmarried.
64 Their priests fell by the sword,
but their widows did not weep.
65 But then the LORD awoke from his sleep;
he was like a warrior in a drunken rage.
66 He drove his enemies back;
he made them a permanent target for insults.
67 He rejected the tent of Joseph;
he did not choose the tribe of Ephraim.
68 He chose the tribe of Judah
and Mount Zion, which he loves.
69 He made his sanctuary as enduring
as the heavens above,
as secure as the earth, which he established permanently.
70 He chose David, his servant,
and took him from the sheepfolds.
71 He took him away from following the mother sheep,
and made him the shepherd of Jacob, his people,
and of Israel, his chosen nation.
72 David cared for them with pure motives;
he led them with skill.

"Use me as Thou wilt, send me where Thou wilt, and work out Thy whole will in my life at any cost now and forever."

Betty Stam

SOAP / *Psalm 77:11–12*
SCRIPTURE / *Write out the SOAP verses*

_____

_____

_____

_____

_____

_____

_____

_____

_____

_____

_____

_____

_____

_____

_____

_____

_____

_____

OBSERVATION / *Write 3 - 4 observations*

_____

_____

_____

_____

_____

_____

APPLICATION / *Write down 1 - 2 applications*

_____
_____
_____
_____
_____
_____
_____
_____
_____
_____
_____

PRAYER / *Write out a prayer over what you learned*

_____
_____
_____
_____
_____
_____
_____
_____
_____
_____
_____
_____
_____
_____
_____
_____

THANKFUL

*Write three things you are thankful for
today and why each one brings you joy.*

ONE

....
....
....
....
....
....
....

TWO

....
....
....
....
....
....
....

THREE

....
....
....
....
....
....
....

Psalm 79

A psalm of Asaph.

1 O God, foreigners have invaded your chosen land;
they have polluted your holy temple
and turned Jerusalem into a heap of ruins.
2 They have given the corpses of your servants
to the birds of the sky,
the flesh of your loyal followers
to the beasts of the earth.
3 They have made their blood flow like water
all around Jerusalem, and there is no one to bury them.
4 We have become an object of disdain to our neighbors;
those who live on our borders taunt and insult us.
5 How long will this go on, O LORD?
Will you stay angry forever?
How long will your rage burn like fire?
6 Pour out your anger on the nations
that do not acknowledge you,
on the kingdoms that do not pray to you.
7 For they have devoured Jacob
and destroyed his home.
8 Do not hold us accountable for the
sins of earlier generations.
Quickly send your compassion our way,
for we are in serious trouble.
9 Help us, O God, our deliverer!
For the sake of your glorious reputation, rescue us.
Forgive our sins for the sake of your reputation.
10 Why should the nations say, "Where is their God?"
Before our very eyes may the shed blood of your servants
be avenged among the nations.
11 Listen to the painful cries of the prisoners.
Use your great strength to set free
those condemned to die.

Psalm 79 (continued)

12 Pay back our neighbors in full.
May they be insulted the same way
they insulted you, O Lord.
13 Then we, your people, the
sheep of your pasture,
will continually thank you.
We will tell coming generations
of your praiseworthy acts.

Psalm 80

*For the music director, according to the
shushan-eduth style; a psalm of Asaph.*

1 O Shepherd of Israel, pay attention,
you who lead Joseph like a flock of sheep.
You who sit enthroned above the
cherubim, reveal your splendor.
2 In the sight of Ephraim, Benjamin,
and Manasseh reveal your power.
Come and deliver us.
3 O God, restore us.
Smile on us. Then we will be delivered.
4 O Lord God of Heaven's Armies,
how long will you remain angry at your
people while they pray to you?
5 You have given them tears as food;
you have made them drink tears by the measure.
6 You have made our neighbors dislike us,
and our enemies insult us.
7 O God of Heaven's Armies, restore us.
Smile on us. Then we will be delivered.

Psalm 80 (continued)

8 You uprooted a vine from Egypt;
you drove out nations and transplanted it.
9 You cleared the ground for it;
it took root,
and filled the land.
10 The mountains were covered by its shadow,
the highest cedars by its branches.
11 Its branches reached the Mediterranean Sea,
and its shoots the Euphrates River.
12 Why did you break down its walls,
so that all who pass by pluck its fruit?
13 The wild boars of the forest ruin it;
the insects of the field feed on it.
14 O God of Heaven's Armies, come back.
Look down from heaven and take notice.
Take care of this vine,
15 the root your right hand planted,
the shoot you made to grow.
16 It is burned and cut down.
May those who did this die because
you are displeased with them.
17 May you give support to the
one you have chosen,
to the one whom you raised up for yourself.
18 Then we will not turn away from you.
Revive us and we will pray to you.
19 O Lord God of Heaven's Armies, restore us.
Smile on us. Then we will be delivered.

SOAP / *Psalm 79:8*
SCRIPTURE / *Write out the SOAP verses*

_____

_____

_____

_____

_____

_____

_____

_____

_____

_____

_____

_____

_____

_____

_____

_____

_____

_____

OBSERVATION / *Write 3 - 4 observations*

_____

_____

_____

_____

_____

_____

APPLICATION / *Write down 1 - 2 applications*

_____

_____

_____

_____

_____

_____

_____

_____

_____

_____

PRAYER / *Write out a prayer over what you learned*

_____

_____

_____

_____

_____

_____

_____

_____

_____

_____

_____

_____

_____

_____

_____

_____

THANKFUL

*Write three things you are thankful for
today and why each one brings you joy.*

ONE

....

....

....

....

....

....

....

TWO

....

....

....

....

....

....

....

THREE

....

....

....

....

....

....

....

Record an application you learned from your SOAP study this week and how you will practically implement it in your life.

....
....
....
....
....
....
....
....
....
....
....
....
....
....
....
....
....
....
....
....
....
....
....
....
....
....

Join Us

ONLINE
lovegodgreatly.com

JOURNALS
lovegodgreatly.com/store

FACEBOOK
lovegodgreatly

INSTAGRAM
@lovegodgreatlyofficial

APP
Love God Greatly

....

CONTACT US
info@lovegodgreatly.com

CONNECT
#LoveGodGreatly

FOR YOU

What we offer

30+ Translations
Bible Reading Plans
Online Bible Study
Love God Greatly App
Over 200 Countries Served
Bible Study Journals
Community Groups
Love God Greatly Bible
Love God Greatly Journal

Each study includes

Three Weekly Blog Posts
Daily Devotions
Memory Verses
Weekly Challenges
Weekly Reflection Questions
Bridge Reading Plan

Other studies

The Gospel of Mark
Everlasting Covenant
Jesus Our Everything
Know Love
Empowered: Yesterday and Today
Risen
Draw Near
Beatitudes
Esther
Words Matter
Walking in Victory
To Do Justice, To Love Kindness, To Walk Humbly
Faithful Love
Choose Brave
Savior
Promises of God
Love the Loveless
Truth Over Lies
1 & 2 Thessalonians
Fear & Anxiety
James

His Name Is...
Philippians
1 & 2 Timothy
Sold Out
Ruth
Broken & Redeemed
Walking in Wisdom
God With Us
In Everything Give Thanks
You Are Forgiven
David
Ecclesiastes
Growing Through Prayer
Names of God
Galatians
Psalm 119
1st & 2nd Peter
Made For Community
The Road To Christmas
The Source Of Gratitude
You Are Loved

www.ingramcontent.com/pod-product-compliance
Lightning Source LLC
Chambersburg PA
CBHW070027100426
42740CB00013B/2612